# The Trainer's
# Support Handbook

# The Trainer's Support Handbook

A Practical Guide to Managing the
Administrative Details of Training

**Jean Barbazette**

**McGraw-Hill**

New York   Chicago   San Francisco   Lisbon
London   Madrid   Mexico City   Milan
New Delhi   San Juan   Seoul
Singapore   Sydney   Toronto

**Library of Congress Control Number**

2001012345

*McGraw-Hill*

*A Division of The **McGraw·Hill** Companies*

2 3 4 5 6 7 8 9 0    1PBT/1PBT    0 9 8 7 6 5 4 3 2 1

ISBN 0-07-137028-5

Printed and bound by Phoenix Book Technology

McGraw-Hill books are available at special quantity discounts to use as premiums and sales promotions, or for use in corporate training sessions. For more information, please write to the Director of Special Sales, Professional Publishing, McGraw-Hill, Two Penn Plaza, New York, NY 10121-2298. Or contact your local bookstore.

 This book is printed on recycled, acid-free paper containing a minimum of 50% recycled, de-inked fiber.

To Richard Barbazette, my husband and business partner, a source of invaluable ideas and projects.

# Contents

## CHAPTER 3

### How to Assess Training Needs

Objectives    *25*

Decide who and what is assessed

Learn how to perform a training assessment

Learn how to conserve training resources and identify training issues

Use a tool to sort training needs from training wants

Use goal analysis to make vague desires specific

Identify who needs training

Help line managers and supervisors identify training needs

Learn what to do with assessment information or how to develop a training plan

Learn how to present a training plan to management and gain approval

Questions    *26*

Chapter Tools

## CHAPTER 4

### How to Select Training Programs and Packages Employees Want to Use

Objectives    *53*

How to select the best resource to provide training

How to buy external training programs

How to participate in buying decisions

Set objectives for training events

Establish requirements to buy packaged training programs and training videos—what does good training look like?

Identify external resources for training programs

Identify criteria to review external training proposals

## CHAPTER 7

## How to Hire a Consultant or External Trainer

## CHAPTER 8

## How to Begin to Market Training Internally

## CHAPTER 9

## How to Publicize Training Events

## CHAPTER 10

### How to Set Up and Maintain Your Company's Training Web Site

## CHAPTER 11

### How to Smoothly Administer Training Events

## CHAPTER 12

## How to Set Up Off-Site Training Events

Objectives   *147*

Negotiate with hotels for off-site meeting rooms

Coordinate off-site facility arrangements

Make travel arrangements for instructors and training participants

## CHAPTER 13

## Set Up and Run a Corporate Resource Center

Objectives   *157*

Maintain a corporate library and/or resource center with up-to-date information

Purchase audiovisual equipment

## CHAPTER 14

## Show Me the Money: Budgeting for Training

## CHAPTER 15

## How to Evaluate and Demonstrate the Success of Training

# Acknowledgments

Thanks to many people who helped research and produce this book: Melissa Smith, Kathleen Terry, Linda Ernst, Carolyn Balling, Maria Chilcote, Karen Palmer, Terri Rodrigues, Kelly Barbazette, Richard Narramore, and Fred Dahl.

# INTRODUCTION

A recent study showed that training professionals spend at least half of their time away from the classroom performing support functions.

Yet there are very few resources available to trainers to help cope with these support duties and responsibilities.

This book is designed to simplify this "neglected other half" of a trainer's responsibilities. It provides dozens of tools, tips, templates, and checklists to make the administrative part of training easier. Most of the tools can be described as helping trainers plan and organize, set up, and follow up after training events.

## TRAINING PRIORITIES CASE STUDY

Melissa was confused about her priorities. There were so many requests for training. Where should she start first? Melissa is the new trainer for a small bank with six branches in local communities. Before Melissa became the bank's only "official" trainer, any training that occurred was informal and done by individual supervisors. Melissa was one of those supervisors, and she ran a superior operation.

As the bank grew, the need arose to standardize procedures and train employees to use standardized procedures for basic jobs: new accounts, teller services, several operations processing jobs, etc. Melissa recruited some of the bank's best subject matter experts to put together training for basic jobs. This has not gone well. The pilot class was mostly lecture with very little "hands-on" training and poor results.

The president mentioned several times that complaints from bank customers were on the rise and there was a need to train all employees in customer-service skills. After calling friends at other banks and searching the Web for resources, Melissa received lots of sales literature and even interviewed three consultants and previewed two customer-service packaged programs. The costs for consultants and programs range from $5,000 to $25,000. Of course, every vendor says his or her company has the best product. She has yet to find time to check references for any of the consultants and programs.

The bank president also gave Melissa responsibility for the annual shareholders' meeting. Most of her time the past month was taken with coordinating the details of the program, sending invitations to shareholders, and making arrangements with the hotel. The hotel Melissa was dealing with for the annual meeting has just canceled all of the bank's meeting space because someone else from the hotel booked a large convention! The meeting is less than one month away.

The controller of the bank has just sent Melissa an e-mail requesting that she put together a training schedule for the new payroll computer system that the bank will install in two months.

With all of these requests for training from several sources, Melissa is feeling stressed, underappreciated, and somewhat powerless to deal with situations beyond her control.

## Does This Sound Like You?

Since 1982, The Training Clinic of Seal Beach, California, has conducted train-the-trainer workshops for more than 140,000 training professionals. Many of these clients report similar struggles: the need to be better organized, prioritize activities; feeling frequently overwhelmed by requests for training activities. Some trainers feel underappreciated and powerless to assert themselves when requests are inappropriate or unrealistic. The case study on the previous page describes a typical trainer. Does any of this sound familiar?

How to deal with these and many other issues and problems is the subject of this book. Chapter 1 offers strategies to prioritize and organize the administrative roles and responsibilities of the training professional. It also includes a variety of checklists to help implement these strategies. Chapter 2 suggests how to gain greater support by management. Chapter 5 provides help to select and coach subject matter experts as internal trainers. Chapters 4 and 7 help the trainer navigate the minefields of using external trainers and consultants and reviewing training proposals and packages. Chapter 12 helps the training coordinator deal with off-site facilities, and Chapter 11 suggests how to schedule training events for maximum attendance.

This book is unique in helping training professionals to become more proactive than reactive in carrying out their administrative responsibilities. Other books may provide functional information, such as meeting planning or budgeting, but none of them addresses the comprehensive needs of the training professional who also has administrative work to do.

## How to Use This Book

Since training professionals have varied support roles and responsibilities, the reader can use all or selected sections of this book, depending on individual needs and which tool is needed for a specific situation. To identify individual needs for the tools discussed in each chapter, read the objectives and complete the questions at the beginning of each chapter to identify your stage of development in each of the skills provided in a chapter. If you are at Stage 1 or Stage 2, you may need to read and use the materials in the entire chapter. If you are operating at Stage 3 or above, a review of the tools provided in the chapter can be a time-saver.

Each chapter provides tools and checklists to develop specific skills that make support responsibilities easier to complete on a routine or one-time basis. All of the questions that begin each chapter are collected in a training department audit in Appendix A. All of the checklists and templates are available and can be downloaded from *www.books.mcgraw-hill.com/training/download*.

*Jean Barbazette*
*Seal Beach, CA*

# The Trainer's
# Support
# Handbook

Chapter 1

# Help! How to Prioritize Training Responsibilities and Keep Your Sanity

## Objectives

- Identify priorities for your job.

- Develop your own job description.

- Identify key roles and responsibilities of training coordinators, and develop personal and department "mission statements."

## Chapter Tools

- Trainer Job Description

- Job Description Template

- Mission Statement Worksheet

## Questions

Answer these two questions to identify your current development level for the issues addressed in this chapter.

1. *Which stage of development describes how priorities are set for the training coordinator?*

   — Stage 1: How to set priorities is unclear. You are reactive and focus on administrative functions. Roles and responsibilities are sometimes unclear and overlap with other areas.

   — Stage 2: You have a written job description and a specific line of reporting authority. Much of your work consists of "other duties as assigned."

   — Stage 3: Your priorities are to act primarily as an internal consultant to management, to find resources for courses, to select and develop internal subject matter experts as trainers, and to select appropriate external trainers and training packages. Your roles and responsibilities are clear to you and others.

   — Stage 4: You do everything described in Stage 3 and find backup instructors to avoid canceling classes during highly active training periods.

   — Stage 5: You do everything described in Stage 4 and also ensure that the function addresses appropriate issues by using continuous improvement methods.

2. *Which stage of development describes the mission and objectives of the training function?*

   — Stage 1: There is no clearly defined mission or business plan. If a mission statement exists, it is not clearly communicated internally to management.

   — Stage 2: The mission and objectives are clearly defined for the staff by upper management and limited to products and/or services.

   — Stage 3: The training function mission and objectives are developed into a training plan.

   — Stage 4: Progress toward achieving the mission and objectives of the training function is regularly assessed.

   — Stage 5: When necessary, the mission and objectives are adjusted based on information from a variety of resources.

If you rated yourself at Stage 1 or Stage 2, you might want to proceed through this chapter as it is written. If you rated yourself at Stage 3 or higher, you might benefit from previewing the tools provided in this chapter before working through the ideas and suggestions provided with the checklists.

The tools, skills, and checklists in this chapter will enable you to operate at a higher level of development. The case study from the introduction, which describes a typical training professional who is having difficulty setting priorities, is repeated here. As you reread the case, try to identify

1. What roles and responsibilities is the training professional, Melissa, being asked to perform?

2. What takes up most of Melissa's time?

3. Where would you advise Melissa to focus her energy?

## TRAINING PRIORITIES CASE STUDY

Melissa is the new trainer for a small bank with six branches in local communities. She is confused about her priorities. There are so many requests for training. Where should she start first?

As the bank grew, the need arose to standardize procedures and train employees to use these procedures for basic jobs: creating new accounts, teller services, operations processing jobs, etc. Melissa recruited some of the bank's best subject matter experts to organize training for basic jobs, but this process is not going well. The pilot class is a lecture with very little "hands-on" training and yields poor results.

The president mentioned several times that complaints from bank customers were on the rise, which indicates a need to provide all employees with training in customer-service skills. After calling friends at other banks and searching the Web for resources, Melissa received lots of sales literature and even interviewed three consultants and previewed two customer-service packaged programs. The costs for consultants and programs range from $5,000 to $25,000. Of course, every vendor says his or her company has the best product. Melissa doesn't have the time to check references for any of the consultants and programs.

The bank president also gave Melissa the responsibility of organizing the annual shareholders' meeting. Most of her time the past month was spent coordinating the details of the program, sending invitations to shareholders, and making hotel arrangements. The hotel Melissa booked for the annual meeting has just canceled all of the bank's meeting space because someone else from the hotel booked a large convention! The meeting is less than one month away.

On top of that, the controller of the bank has just sent Melissa an e-mail requesting that she put together a training schedule for the new payroll computer system that the bank will install in two months.

With all of these requests for training from several sources, Melissa is feeling stressed, underappreciated, and somewhat powerless to deal with situations that seem beyond her control.

Here are suggested answers to the three questions above.

1. What roles and responsibilities is Melissa being asked to perform?

    — Standardize how basic jobs are done

    — Provide training on basic jobs

    — Coordinate the annual shareholder's meeting, including troubleshooting canceled hotel space

    — Provide customer-service skills training

    — Schedule training for the new payroll computer system

2. What takes most of this trainer's time?

    — Planning and troubleshooting for the annual meeting

3. Where would you advise Melissa to focus her energy?

    — Develop a job description and gain approval from top management for her administrative roles and responsibilities. Her administrative role and responsibilities need to be aligned with the needs of the bank. The mission of the training function needs to be developed, approved, and published for all in the organization to see.

    — Assess the training needs for operations, customer service, and the payroll computer system. Some of these requests for training may not require training as a solution to a performance problem.

    — Put together a training plan to meet the training needs.

    — Get management's buy-in for the plan. This means Melissa will have access to management along with their support for the development of the bank's employees.

    — Develop a strategy to deal with being under appreciated, powerless, and stressed. Much of this strategy should include building a partnership with those who deliver training. She can develop her own expertise and help others deliver state-of-the-art training by keeping up with training trends.

## Set Priorities and Keep Your Sanity

The five suggestions in the preceding list regarding where Melissa should focus her energy are good recommendations for any training professional who wants to be more focused and to take a more proactive approach in carrying out her administrative responsibilities. A new job description will help clarify priorities and gain support for her day-to-day activities. To create a new job description, use the list of support activities starting on page 6. There is a job description template on page 8.

A mission statement can be developed based on the day-to-day activities the training professional performs. If the current activities and mission need to be redirected, this is an opportunity to describe what the training function can become. Once a picture of the future of the training function is clear, a new mission statement can be developed that is aimed at realizing the future. Tools to develop a mission statement are presented starting on page 10.

Assessing the training needs will help keep the training professional focused on providing training as a solution to issues that require one. Some suggested analysis tools can be found in Chapter 3 to help the training coordinator clarify training needs.

How to put together a training plan is addressed at the end of Chapter 3. Once a training solution is deemed appropriate, the training professional can offer assistance in developing a training plan that meets the needs of those requesting training.

Getting management's buy-in for the plan is an essential part of any plan because it helps the training professional stay focused and be successful. Getting management's buy-in means that the training professional has access to management. Tools to gain access to management and get their buy-in appear in Chapter 2.

The fifth suggestion, develop a strategy to deal with being under appreciated, powerless and stressed, will help keep the training professional proactive, focused and results oriented. Tools to connect with those who deliver training as well as strategies to continue personal development and keeping up with training trends can be found in Chapter 2.

## Write the Job Description

Once the administrative duties and responsibilities of the training professional are identified, they can be drafted into a job description. A job description that states the primary purpose of the position along with major job objectives and prioritized responsibilities and activities clarifies expectations for the training professional and those who interact with him or her. The job description needs approval from management to ensure that the training coordinator's roles and responsibilities are aligned with the business needs of the organization. Circulating the job description among those who work with the training professional will help clarify expectations when multiple demands on the training professional's time arise.

# TRAINER JOB DESCRIPTION

**Directions:** Identify which of the following administrative roles and responsibilities best reflect your current or desired position. What percentage of the trainer's time should be spent outside the classroom and not involved in designing or presenting training programs?

## Section 1: Trainer Roles and Responsibilities

Identify the amount of time spent on each of these activities:

__ Designing training programs

__ Presenting classroom or on-the-job training

__ Building a team with those who provide training in the organization

__ Participating in human resource planning to meet business needs

__ Handling training administration details (meeting set-up, scheduling, confirmation, materials duplication, order supplies, etc.)

__ Marketing training internally

__ Keeping statistics about the events and performance for training in the organization

__ Preparing and monitoring the training budget or participating in buying and budgeting decisions

__ Evaluating the effectiveness of training done in the organization

## Section 2: Tasks, Skills, and Abilities

Which of the following knowledge or skills are needed for the training professional's roles and responsibilities?

__ Identify training issues related to a business need

__ Distinguish between training needs and wants

__ Help line managers/supervisors identify training needs

__ Get management support for training solutions

__ Help supervisors and managers set performance standards

__ Identify who needs training

__ Establish criteria to measure the results of training

__ Identify the cost of training

__ Select the best resource to provide training

__ Present a training plan to management and gain approval

---

\_\_ Set objectives for training events

\_\_ Identify external resources for training programs

\_\_ Establish criteria for buying packaged training programs and training videos

\_\_ Identify criteria for reviewing external training proposals

\_\_ Interview, select, negotiate with, hire, and monitor external consultants

\_\_ Select subject matter experts who will conduct training

\_\_ Coach subject matter experts to deliver training

\_\_ Maintain a corporate library and/or resource center with up-to-date information

\_\_ Purchase training equipment (projectors, hardware, software, etc.)

\_\_ Select and administer assessment instruments or inventories

\_\_ Prepare training announcements, course catalogs, and brochures

\_\_ Create benefit statements to help "sell" training internally

\_\_ Create a partnership with supervisors to avoid "no shows" at training events

\_\_ Create newsletters, bulletin boards, and e-mail training announcements

\_\_ Use a variety of methods to publicize training events

\_\_ Use data collection and graphics to demonstrate training results

\_\_ Use recognition tools for those who support training

\_\_ Publicize the variety of services available from the training function

\_\_ Conduct evaluation with supervisors following training events

\_\_ Use marketing information to develop future training plans

\_\_ Run trainee registration and confirmation systems

\_\_ Monitor tuition reimbursement programs

\_\_ Schedule training

\_\_ Prepare training rooms for instruction

\_\_ Negotiate with hotels for off-site meeting rooms

\_\_ Make travel arrangements for instructors and training participants

\_\_ Coordinate off-site facility arrangements

\_\_ Set a standard (style guide) for printed training materials

\_\_ Duplicate and inventory training materials

\_\_ Order training supplies and maintain audio-visual equipment

## JOB DESCRIPTION TEMPLATE

Use the "Trainer Job Description" task list on the previous pages to identify current or desired roles and responsibilities and job tasks and skills.

## Roles and Responsibilities and Percent of Time for Each

## Job Tasks

## Job Skills

Identify the percent of time spent on each activity. Gain your manager's agreement on the priorities reflected here.

## Mission Statement

Once the job description is developed and a clearer picture of the training function's activities is visible, the mission of the training function will become clearer. The mission of the training function is the "business" conducted by the function. If the training function has no formal mission statement, looking at what the training function has been doing can reveal an implicit mission. For example, if the major responsibilities of the training professional have been to enroll new employees in outside training courses when requested, then the training function's mission could be, *"to locate workshops that will increase the skills of new employees."*

Or, for example, if the major responsibilities of the training professional have been to find internal subject matter experts to train new employees on essential skills, the training function's mission could be, *"to increase skills of new employees by providing essential job-related skills."*

For clarity, it is appropriate to write a mission statement based on the current roles and responsibilities of the training function. If that mission does not reflect a training function that meets business objectives, then a mission statement can be written as a vision of what the training function needs to be.

## MISSION STATEMENT WORKSHEET

What are the major activities conducted in your training department?

Based on these activities, identify the collective purpose of these activities. Write the purpose (mission) statement in one sentence.

## Objectives

- Determine how to partner with line managers.

- Identify strategies to gain access to management.

- Find out how to keep up to date and avoid "flavor of the month" training.

- Develop a strategy to deal with being under appreciated, powerless and stressed.

## Chapter Tools

- Develop a Partnership Between Managers/Supervisors and the Training Department

- Partnership Checklist for Management

- Partnership Checklist for the Training Department

- Great Expectations

- Sample Checklist Summary of Skills from Customer Service Skills Workshop

- Sample Skills Observation Checklist

- Sample Supervisor's Help Action Plan

- Sample Action Plan Making This Work for You.

Chapter 2

# How to Get Support for the Training Department

## Questions

Answer these four questions to identify the development level for the issues addressed in this chapter.

1. *Describe the level of access and support for training from upper management.*

   __ Stage 1: The training department operates on a reactive basis to assist upper management with immediate operational requests.

   __ Stage 2: The training department takes initial steps to gain access to management to support individual training events with minimal planning.

   __ Stage 3: Management is accessible on a regular basis to the training department and those who train. Management shows a real interest in training and often introduces training events.

   __ Stage 4: Management is accessible and supportive of training projects.

   __ Stage 5: Management is directly accessible and supportive and participates as a sponsor for training department projects.

2. *Describe how well you keep up to date with training trends.*

   __ Stage 1: I have no awareness of training trends.

   __ Stage 2: I have minimal awareness of training trends.

   __ Stage 3: Trend updates are pursued on an individual basis.

   __ Stage 4: Training trends are systematically studied and followed where appropriate.

   __ Stage 5: Training trends updates are integrated into doing business. The training department is a trendsetter and may participate in trend research. Planning helps to avoid negative consequences of impending trends.

3. *Describe the level of support for trainers to participate in professional organizations.*

   __ Stage 1: Little or no support exists for membership in outside professional organizations.

   __ Stage 2: Attendance at outside training and professional meetings is limited due to work pressure.

   __ Stage 3: Training professionals occasionally attend outside professional development sessions and share that information with colleagues.

   __ Stage 4: Training professionals regularly attend outside professional development sessions and share that information with colleagues.

   __ Stage 5: Active membership in professional organizations is normal. Trainers are trendsetters among their peers and give presentations at professional conferences.

4. *Describe the level of decision-making authority and appreciation expressed by management for the duties and responsibilities of the training department.*

   __ Stage 1: Management gives little to no decision-making authority along with training responsibilities.

   __ Stage 2: Management gives minor decision-making authority along with training responsibilities.

__ Stage 3: Management gives regular training related decision-making authority to the training department for routine responsibilities. Training professionals make recommendations for how to handle new responsibilities.

__ Stage 4: Management gives regular training-related decision-making authority to training professionals for all responsibilities and seeks approval for unusual decisions.

__ Stage 5: Management gives all training-related decision-making authority to the training department. The training professional reports exceptions to management after the event has passed.

If you rated yourself at Stage 1 or Stage 2 for most of these diagnostic questions, you might want to proceed through this chapter as it is written. If you rated yourself at Stage 3 or higher, you might benefit from previewing the tools provided in this chapter before working through the ideas and suggestions provided with the checklists.

## Get Management Buy-In

When training professionals build a partnership with management, it is easier to gain access and support for the training function. The partners also share decision-making responsibility, which alleviates the stress that sometimes stems from feeling underappreciated and powerless.

The chart on page 14 shows a suggested partnership between management and the training function. It describes the responsibilities of each partner at four different times: when training is planned, prepared, presented, and following training events. Joint planning of training events means that management has established standards of performance for those who will be trained. Training needs are jointly defined, the training professional does a target population analysis with support from management, and expectations and learning objectives are agreed upon.

During the preparation of the training program, the trainer develops content that meets the objectives and provides an overview or pilot session so managers and supervisors can become familiar with the content of the training. See the list of suggestions for how to introduce the training program to employees and set appropriate expectations that starts on page 18. Schedule the training on mutually convenient dates. See Chapter 11 for scheduling techniques and suggestions.

During the training, the management partner agrees to assure attendance of employees, and to not interrupt the training; in return, the training partner will address issues and problems and how to apply new skills back on the job. Some type of evaluation will take place to ensure that learning objectives are met. Chapter 15 offers suggestions to evaluate learning. The management partner also needs to prepare the work environment to be conducive to new learning by removing obstacles. For example, if software training is provided, the software should be installed on the employee's desktop computer before or during training. If possible, management needs to compensate for the backlog in the workload while employees are at training by either sharing work with others or providing substitute or temporary employees during training. Sometimes, it is appropriate to reduce production goals during training when employees are not at their normal workstations. Training becomes less attractive to employees who work overtime to catch up on missed work.

# DEVELOP A PARTNERSHIP BETWEEN MANAGERS/SUPERVISORS AND THE TRAINING DEPARTMENT

|  | Manager and Supervisor Roles | Training Department Roles |
|---|---|---|
| **Planning** | • Set standards of performance<br>• Define and assess training needs with trainer<br>• Define the target population<br>• Establish expectations and objectives with the trainer | • Help the manager define performance standards if none exist<br>• Define and assess training needs with supervisor<br>• Analyze the target population<br>• Set expectations and objectives with the supervisor |
| **Preparation** | • Become familiar with program content<br>• Introduce employees to the training program<br>• Communicate the need for training to the employee<br>• Clarify expectations with the employee following training | • Develop program content to meet agreed-upon objectives<br>• Provide an overview/pilot of the training program for supervisors/managers<br>• Schedule training with considerations for workload and the organization's needs |
| **Presentation** | • Assure attendance of scheduled employees<br>• Do not interrupt the training<br>• Prepare the work environment to use new learning<br>• Compensate for the workload while employees are at training | • Address issues and problems<br>• Stress application of new skills to the job<br>• Evaluate whether learning took place and learning objectives were met |
| **Follow-Up** | • Meet with the employee to discuss new knowledge, skills, and attitudes (KSA) developed from training<br>• Provide follow-up coaching and positive reinforcement<br>• Remove work environment obstacles to applying new learning<br>• Include new KSA in performance appraisal<br>• Participate with trainers to evaluate the results of training | • Provide information to supervisors to assist in follow-up coaching and support<br>• Validate content by observing employees use new skills on the job<br>• Evaluate the results of changed behavior with supervisors<br>• Review and revise training as needed |

During the follow-up phase, the training partner provides supervisors with information to coach and support new learning. A summary of skills, a copy of an action plan, or an on-the-job checklist provides supervisors with a way of measuring the transfer of new learning to the job. Sample summary of skills checklists, sample action plans, and on-the-job checklists appear starting on page 20. Chapter 16 describes how to develop summary of skills and on-the-job checklists.

The management partner should meet with the employee to discuss how new knowledge, skills, and attitudes can be implemented on the job. Observations with checklists will reinforce new learning. The training partner can provide coaching skills for the supervisors and managers and recommend ways to positively reinforce new learning. If managers have not removed obstacles to implementing new learning while training took place, now is the time to do so. When the management partner holds employees accountable for new learning by measuring it during a performance appraisal, there is a better chance that new learning will become a regular way of doing a job. Both partners also need to evaluate the results of training and revise the training, if needed. Chapter 16 suggests ways to measure the results of training.

# PARTNERSHIP CHECKLIST
# FOR MANAGEMENT

*Use this checklist for managers to appropriately support a specific training event. Duplicate this form and provide it to managers with each training event to clearly identify management responsibilities for training.*

**When planning a training event, the manager needs to**

- Set standards of performance

- Define and assess training needs with trainer

- Define the target population

- Establish expectations and objectives with the trainer

**When preparing for a training event, the manager needs to**

- Become familiar with program content

- Introduce employees to the training program

- Communicate the need for training to employees

- Clarify expectations with employees following training

**During the training event, the manager needs to**

- Assure attendance of scheduled employees

- Not interrupt the training

- Prepare the work environment to use new learning

- Compensate for the workload while employees are at training

**Following the training event, the manager needs to**

- Meet with each employee to discuss new knowledge, skills, and attitudes (KSA) developed from training

- Provide follow-up coaching and positive reinforcement

- Remove work environment obstacles to applying new learning

- Include new KSA in performance appraisal

- Participate with trainers to evaluate the results of training

# PARTNERSHIP CHECKLIST FOR THE TRAINING DEPARTMENT

*Use this checklist for the training department to appropriately support a specific training event. Duplicate this form and provide it to trainers with each training event to clearly identify training department responsibilities for training.*

**When planning a training event, the training department needs to**

- Help the manager define performance standards if none exist

- Define and assess training needs with supervisor

- Analyze the target population

- Set expectations and objectives with the supervisor

**When preparing for a training event, the training department needs to**

- Develop program content to meet agreed-upon objectives

- Provide an overview/pilot of the training program for supervisors and managers

- Schedule training with considerations for workload and the organization's needs

**During the training event, the training department needs to**

- Address real issues and problems

- Stress application of new skills to the job

- Evaluate whether learning took place and learning objectives were met

**Following the training event, the training department needs to**

- Provide information to supervisors to assist in follow-up coaching and support

- Validate content by observing employees use new skills on the job

- Evaluate the results of changed behavior with supervisors

- Review and revise training as needed

# GREET EXPECTATIONS

Use the following suggestions to assist internal clients in getting the most from on-site workshops and make the event a successful, productive learning experience. Provide this summary of expectations and suggestions to management along with a written confirmation letter that describes logistics and event details. The specific workshop referenced in this form is "Meeting Planning."

## Before the Training

1. Review the outline and objectives that have been written to reflect your issues. Are there changes that should be made?

2. Meet with the participants and discuss what you see as the business need and the trends in the organization that are being met by their attendance at this course.

   — Write an invitation or announcement to the participants you expect to attend this workshop.

   — Write benefit statements (in addition to the objectives) describing how your organization and individual participants will benefit from the skills learned in the workshop.

   — Provide participants a copy of the outline with the objectives.

   This workshop should not come as a surprise. Issues about reluctant participation should surface well before the training takes place.

3. Tell participants what you expect following their attendance at this course.

   — How will they be held accountable for using these new skills?

   — What materials will they facilitate?

   — When will they facilitate?

   — Will using these new skills be observed or reviewed on a performance appraisal?

   — How will they be acknowledged and credited for their contribution?

4. Class hours are usually from 8:30 a.m. to 4:30 p.m. Do these hours need to be adjusted to meet your work hours? Earlier starting and finishing times are possible. We will need an overhead projector, flip chart with paper, and a screen. A "U" shape setting is best for a group of less than 20.

## During the Training

5. Participants should be prepared to participate and attend the workshop for the entire day. Phone calls and messages need to be handled only at breaks (one in the morning, lunchtime, and one in the afternoon). To the extent possible, compensate for workload while the employee is at training.

6. As the manager or supervisor, we need your participation at the workshop for the entire day. Your presence will impart a stronger message than anything we can say about the importance of learning

these new skills. We would appreciate your beginning the workshop and restating the business need that prompted the workshop and what objectives you have for the training function.

7. It would be a good idea for the entire group to have lunch together. This will help us keep to the time constraints and allow the instructor to have some informal time with the participants.

## Following the Training

8. As a follow-up, give the participants a week or two to complete the development of their meeting plan.

9. Have the group meet together and ask each person to present what he or she has planned.

— Ask the group to critique the plan and offer suggestions to ensure that the meeting will be interactive and meets the stated objectives.

— Participants may benefit from facilitating a portion of their plan and getting feedback from the group. This is a good opportunity to try out their plan.

10. Have the group meet again after participants have been able to try out their facilitation skills. Celebrate successes, and discuss ways of handling any problems that may have arisen.

# SAMPLE CHECKLIST SUMMARY OF SKILLS
# FROM CUSTOMER SERVICE SKILLS WORKSHOP

Manager/Supervisor: Use this checklist to observe how often the learner uses these behaviors following training:

1 = rarely           3 = often

2 = sometimes        4 = almost always

Communication styles

\_\_\_\_\_ tries to match the customer's communication style (visual, auditory, kinesthetic) by using language that mirrors the customer's words

Overcome listening barriers

\_\_\_\_\_ listens for facts and feelings

\_\_\_\_\_ acknowledges feelings

\_\_\_\_\_ acknowledges facts

\_\_\_\_\_ avoids jargon

\_\_\_\_\_ avoids trigger words

\_\_\_\_\_ paraphrases to understand clearly

Tone of voice

\_\_\_\_\_ tone matches intention

Feedback

\_\_\_\_\_ describes by using "I" statements (not "you" statements)

\_\_\_\_\_ avoids "always" and "never"

\_\_\_\_\_ is specific, not general

\_\_\_\_\_ focuses on behavior the customer can do something about

Use questions appropriately

\_\_\_\_\_ closed questions to get specific, limited information

\_\_\_\_\_ closed questions to control the conversation

\_\_\_\_\_ open questions to encourage the customer to tell the story

\_\_\_\_\_ open questions to encourage the customer to calm down

\_\_\_\_\_ follow-up questions to get complete information

# SAMPLE SKILL OBSERVATION CHECKLIST

*Directions: As you observe your subordinate employee during the week following training, complete this form. Give the employee feedback on his or her performance. Rate each step or task using the scale below. Often the performance standard is given in the checklist item.*

1 = did not complete this step

2 = partially did the step, not to standard

3 = did the step, completed the standard

4 = did the step, exceeded the standard

_____ 1. Greeted the customer appropriately, giving employee's name and title

_____ 2. Asked open questions appropriately to get complete information

_____ 3. Asked closed questions appropriately to control the conversation

_____ 4. Gave correct information regarding troubleshooting

_____ 5. Made appropriate acknowledging statements in response to the customer's complaint

_____ 6. Did not promise undeliverable service

_____ 7. Was courteous and polite

_____ 8. Handled customer's negative reactions appropriately

_____ 9. Used appropriate closing comments

_____ 10. Completed the call within required time limit

Identify any additional comments to improve the performance of this employee when dealing with this type of call.

# SAMPLE SUPERVISOR'S HELP ACTION PLAN

*The employee completes this plan during the workshop and shares it with the supervisor as part of the post-training discussion between the employee and the supervisor.*

1. Tools—I feel okay about

    1.

    2.

    3.

    4.

2. Tools—I would like to use

    1.

    2.

    3.

    4.

3. Tools—How I plan to use them

    1.

    2.

    3.

    4.

4. Ways my supervisor can support and help reinforce

    1.

    2.

    3.

    4.

## SAMPLE ACTION PLAN
## MAKING THIS WORK FOR YOU

*Employees complete this action plan throughout the workshop and share it back on the job with the supervisor.*

 Insights or ideas?

 Areas to investigate?

 Actions to take?

## A Final Strategy

Building a partnership with line managers has many desirable results. The final suggestion in the case study of Melissa, the trainer, is to develop a strategy to deal with feeling underappreciated, powerless, and stressed. Building a partnership like the one described on page 14 clarifies expectations and reduces the feelings of powerlessness and stress. If the trainer is feeling underappreciated, perhaps it is because others are not aware of how the training function contributes to the organization's objectives. When trainers publicize the results and accomplishments of the function, their efforts are more appreciated by others. Chapter 15 describes how to measure the results of training, and Chapter 9 describes how to publicize training department accomplishments.

Chapter 1 gives suggestions for developing a job description. Clarifying a training coordinator's roles and responsibilities can reduce stress by facilitating the understanding of priorities and the meeting of expectations.

Information is power. Participation in decision making will increase with accurate information. Chapter 3 describes how to assess training needs to proactively develop a training plan, rather than wait for training issues to bubble to the surface as problems.

Finally, continue your own professional development and be alert to training trends. Appendix B lists professional organizations and other resources to help you stay current on training and development issues.

## Chapter 3

# How to Assess Training Needs

## Objectives

- Decide who and what is assessed.

- Learn how to perform a training assessment.

- Learn how to conserve training resources and identify training issues.

- Use a tool to sort training needs from training wants.

- Use goal analysis to make vague desires specific.

- Identify who needs training.

- Help line managers and supervisors identify training needs.

- Learn what to do with assessment information or how to develop a training plan.

- Learn how to present a training plan to management and gain approval.

## Chapter Tools

- Questions for Identifying Information Barriers

- Questions for Identifying Work Environment Barriers

- Questions for Identifying Individual Barriers

- Prioritize Training Needs Sample Supervisory Development Analysis

- Prioritize Training Decision Checklist

- Goal Analysis Checklist

- Target Population Analysis Decision Checklist

- Training Plan Template Checklist

## Questions

Answer these five questions to identify the development level for issues addressed in this chapter.

1. *What is assessed and how?*

   — Stage 1: No clear process to assess needs is evident.

   — Stage 2: Tasks are analyzed to determine the appropriate way to teach a task. Performance analysis is used. Training needs are sorted from training wants.

   — Stage 3: Learning needs of a target population are identified with client involvement. Goal analysis is used to clarify vague training needs. Course materials and appropriate training methodologies are linked to the needs of the target population.

   — Stage 4: Course materials and methodologies are appropriate and valid.

   — Stage 5: There is strong cooperation between the client and the training department to integrate business needs, training needs, specific targets, and job standards.

2. *How is needs assessment performed?*

   — Stage 1: Scheduling of existing training courses substitutes for needs assessment.

   — Stage 2: Task analysis is done to teach a standardized process.

   — Stage 3: A resource requirements analysis is done to identify the most cost-effective and appropriate method(s) to present training.

   — Stage 4: The needs for new learning and course updates are reviewed on a scheduled basis. Line managers are taught how to assess training needs and regularly share information with the training department.

   — Stage 5: There is strong cooperation between the client and the training department to integrate business needs, training needs, specific targets, and job standards.

3. *What is the product of the assessment and how are assessments tied to business needs?*

   — Stage 1: A schedule of training events is created. No specific tie to a business need is evident.

   — Stage 2: Clear learning outcomes are identified and tied to how a job is done.

   — Stage 3: A training plan is developed to include clearly defined business issues that require support from training. Training needs and wants are sorted, and a means to evaluate the training is recommended.

   — Stage 4: Executives are interviewed regularly to identify business needs that require the support of training and for long-term objectives.

   — Stage 5: There is strong cooperation between the client and the training department to integrate business needs, training needs, specific targets, and job standards.

4. *What is the training professional's role in needs assessment?*

— Stage 1: None.

— Stage 2: The trainer attends client's staff meetings to stay current on impending needs and to identify future needs.

— Stage 3: The trainer acts as an internal consultant and identifies how needs have changed over time and identifies new needs.

— Stage 4: The training professional acts as an internal consultant and systematically identifies how needs have changed and identifies new needs.

— Stage 5: There is strong cooperation between the client and the training department to integrate business needs, training needs, specific targets, and job standards.

5. *What is the extent of planning for training?*

— Stage 1: None.

— Stage 2: Training needs and wants are sorted. The training professional helps the operation identify training needs.

— Stage 3: A training plan is completed in response to specific requests and covers conducting one or a few training programs. Training costs are identified and more than one resource is identified for selection of the best alternative.

— Stage 4: A training plan is created for a year at a time, in response to a variety of training requests, that anticipates training needs.

— Stage 5: Training partners with operations to identify training needs that are tied to business needs. The annual planning process has input from operations, training, and customers.

If you rated yourself at Stage 1 or Stage 2 for most of these diagnostic questions, you might want to proceed through this chapter as it is written. If you rated yourself at Stage 3 or higher, you might benefit from previewing the tools provided in this chapter before working through the ideas and suggestions provided with the checklists.

## Training Needs Analysis

To become more proactive, a trainer should gather information about training needs. This strategy helps the training professional focus on priorities, clarify expectations, and become more involved in decision making. Four types of analysis tools follow: performance analysis, goal analysis, needs versus wants analysis, and target population analysis. Each type of analysis is designed to gather different information to determine how to meet a performance need through training.

## Performance Analysis

The purpose of performance analysis is to determine if a performance discrepancy or problem performance is due to a skill deficiency. If skill is lacking, then the problem performance is a training issue. If there is no skill deficiency, the problem performance may be due to inadequate supervision or lack of motivation and needs other solutions.

There are several formal and informal methods for conducting a performance analysis. You will find an informal method to conduct a performance analysis below.[1] This method asks two questions: (1) Is the person able to do the task? (2) Is the person willing to do the task? Based on the answers to these two questions, four possible types of solution are suggested in the following figure.

## Simplified Performance Analysis

|  | **CAN DO IT** | **CAN'T DO IT** |
|---|---|---|
| **WILLING TO DO IT** | **Solution 1**<br><br>This situation can be improved with further support to the person who is supposed to do the task. Support, along with time and resources, will improve performance. | **Solution 2**<br><br>To be successful, the willing person needs<br><br>• Skills training<br><br>• On-the-job training<br><br>• Coaching<br><br>• Resources |
| **WON'T DO IT** | **Solution 3**<br><br>Since the person is capable but won't do the task, ask if the problem is<br><br>• Poor attitude?<br><br>• Lack of consequences?<br><br>• Lack of feedback?<br><br>• Lack of coaching?<br><br>• Lack of practice? | **Solution 4**<br><br>Since the person is currently incapable and unwilling to do the task, ask if the problem is<br><br>• Lack of skills?<br><br>• Poor attitude?<br><br>• Poor supervision?<br><br>• Lack of value?<br><br>• Other problem? |

Providing training to improve performance is appropriate only if the person needs skill improvement and is willing to do the job (solution 2). Several other strategies should be considered along with training if the solution (2 or 4) is on the right side of this matrix. If the solution is on the left side of the matrix (1 or 3), training is not the solution to improving performance.

[1]© 1995 Carolyn Balling and Jean Barbazette. Used with permission.

To further understand how to apply this model of informal performance analysis, read the case study below and answer these two questions:

1. Who are appropriate individuals to interview to find out more about this situation?

2. What questions should be asked to identify whether there is a training problem?

---

### PERFORMANCE ANALYSIS CASE STUDY

The Manager of Information Services (IS) has called you and requested a "Time Management" workshop for all analysts, operators, programmers, and three supervisors (about 16 people). When you ask for more information about the problem, you learn that co-workers often complain about people on the other 12-hour shift. Each shift seems defensive and thinks they are working "hard" enough. User problems are not being resolved in a timely manner. It's difficult to pick up the slack for others when they are not there. The supervisors work 8-hour shifts. Analysts, programmers, and operators work 12-hour shifts for 3 days and have 3 days off. Lead analysts, programmers, and operators are acting supervisors on Saturdays. IS is a 6 day a week, 24 hour a day operation.

The IS manager wants his employees to work "smarter" not "harder"; hence, the request for a "Time Management" workshop. He believes the workload to be realistic. The manager does not want to upset the employees by changing shift hours.

---

### Case Study Answers

Suggested people to interview might include:

- Information services manager

- Weekday supervisors

- Lead people who supervise on the weekends

- A few analysts, programmers, and operators

"Can/can't" questions to ask could include:

- If employees think they are working "hard enough," what work is not getting done?

- What are examples of the difficulties created by "others" not being there?

- What is an example of working "smarter, not harder"?

- Are employees personally disorganized and therefore unable to manage their time well?

- Why are employees unable to solve a user problem in the expected amount of time? Do they lack skill?

- What is the usual amount of time it takes to resolve a user problem?

"Won't/will" questions to ask could include:

- Are employees expected to share work between their shifts?

- Are employees unwilling or unable to share work between shifts?

- What are the barriers to solving the user problems?

Several of these questions use the "can/can't will/won't" model of performance analysis presented on page 28. Additional questions to ask when conducting a performance analysis are arranged in three categories: information barriers, work environment barriers, and individual barriers. Use the following three checklists of suggested questions for each of the three categories.

# QUESTIONS FOR IDENTIFYING
# INFORMATION BARRIERS

*Use these questions to identify barriers to performing as expected that concern having the correct information to complete a task.*

- Does the employee have complete information?

- Is the information accurate?

- Is the information changing rapidly or is it stable?

- Is information acquired in a timely manner?

- Does the employee get feedback when information is incorrect?

- Is there a specific, written current policy the employee can use to guide how the task is done?

- Are employees given conflicting assignments or conflicting information?

- Is the task unnecessarily complex?

- Does the task duplicate work done by others? How is information about duplicate work discovered and shared?

# QUESTIONS FOR IDENTIFYING
# WORK ENVIRONMENT BARRIERS

*Use these questions to identify barriers to performing as expected that concern having inadequate resources, incentives or work methods.*

- Are there enough personnel resources to complete the task?

- Are there enough space, equipment, materials, and supplies to complete the task as expected?

- Are administrative services adequate?

- What are the consequences of doing work as expected?

- What are the consequences of not doing work as expected?

- Are materials and work methods up to date?

- Are deadlines reasonable?

- Are reporting structures clear to the employee and others?

- Is there an agreed-upon decision-making process? Is it used consistently by all employees?

- Is there extensive or unreasonable paperwork?

# QUESTIONS FOR IDENTIFYING INDIVIDUAL BARRIERS

*Sometimes an individual employee is aware of barriers that make it difficult to complete a task as expected. Use these questions to identify personal barriers.*

- Does the employee lack the strength, dexterity, or stamina to complete the task as expected?

- Can the employee concentrate long enough to complete the task?

- Are the rewards for doing the task as expected of interest to the employee?

- Are the employee's personal values consistent with the mission of the department?

- Does the employee take the initiative as expected?

- Does the employee have specific, measurable, and realistic goals?

- Does the employee have the knowledge and skills to complete the task as expected?

### How to Use The Answers

After getting answers to these questions, the training professional can discuss with the IS manager the need to conduct any type of training. This case is based on a real-life situation. As the real IS manager answered many of these questions, it became clear that work standards for responding to user requests needed refinement and were to be shared with all shifts. Inter-shift communication needed to be improved and a clear procedure to manage projects and requests implemented. After much discussion, the IS manager decided that once work standards were established, project management training would be appropriate to establish a common method of working on user requests. The IS manager's request for time management training turned out to be a symptom, not the cause of poor performance.

Any trainer can use a tool, such as performance analysis, to respond to requests for training in an appropriate way, and is more likely to provide a better solution once true causes of poor performance are identified. This approach will help conserve the resources of the training function and clarify a trainer's roles and responsibilities.

For resources on how to conduct a more formal performance analysis, see the bibliography.

## Needs vs. Wants Analysis

Another tool is to sort training needs from training "wants." Often employees request training that they desire for personal betterment that may not be tied to a business need. If an organization sponsors training, there should be a business justification for it. The following survey method is a helpful tool to determine if training "wants" are really training needs for a group of employees. Later in the chapter, you will find a questionnaire for individual employees to complete that will help tie the request to a business need.

### Purpose

This type of survey is intended to identify and prioritize training needs that are related to the organization's business. Training is linked to the bottom line; conducting training will benefit the individual as well as the organization.

### When to Use the Survey

It is often difficult for individual employees to distinguish between training they need to improve specific skill areas that are related to business and training they want that fills other personal needs. For example, an individual might want to take a course in computer graphics, but may not have an opportunity to use this skill in his or her current job. It is easy for an employee to prioritize perceived training needs for himself or herself and others.

## How to Use the Survey

It is most appropriate to survey more than two levels in the organization. Identify one level of employees who represent the appropriate target audience for skill development, such as front-line supervisors.

Ask the supervisors what skills they need to meet their current responsibilities and what skills their peer group needs to complete their responsibilities. It might also be appropriate to ask the subordinates of those supervisors and perhaps their managers the same questions.

It is not unusual for supervisors and their subordinates to identify the same need, but to name it something different. In the example that follows, supervisors and their peers suggest that improvement in training subordinates is a skill they lack and is therefore a training need. The subordinates recommended that supervisors be given training in how to delegate to subordinates. When supervisors were asked why they didn't delegate to subordinates more frequently, they said that their subordinates needed training because they lacked skills to complete tasks that would have been delegated. Both levels of employees surveyed were describing the same issue, but from a different perspective.

When more than two groups express the same perspective, they are more likely to identify training priorities than a single group. Training "wants" or personal desires are easily spotted, and true training priorities can be addressed.

The survey on page 37 is one tool that can be used to assess the training needs of a specific group; in this case, the group consists of supervisors. The narrative data that follows consists of comments from the supervisor's subordinates. The table on page 39 summarizes the survey results and identifies the top three or four most requested courses (priorities).

The trainer should try to identify which are true training priorities and which are "wants" that should not receive scarce training resources.

First, identify the target population that wants training. Through a small sample of individual interviews or group interviews, ask the target group to identify what types of training they would find useful to them. Then survey the rest of the group using the following questionnaire to validate the suggestions of this small sampling of potential trainees.

This survey method has been used successfully with one target population of fewer than 30 supervisors, and another target population of approximately 100 managers. In each situation, a small sample group was interviewed and asked whether specific types of training would be helpful to them and their peer group. If the target population is more than 100, surveying 25 to 50 percent of the group will probably be sufficient to provide useful information. Also, it is important to include only training topics on the list of courses that the organization is prepared to offer. Listing any course on a survey creates the expectation that if enough supervisors select that course, it will be offered and employees will have an opportunity to attend the training.

The survey on page 37 was given to the supervisors or managers along with a 25-word content description of each training program. Supervisors or managers were asked to identify their first three choices (training priorities) in each of three categories of training: personal skills, interpersonal skills, and management skills. A similar survey about their supervisor or manager was provided to the subordinates of the supervisors or managers for completion. Sample survey results follow the survey instrument.

The inventories were completed anonymously. Supervisors and their subordinates were told that their information would be kept anonymous but not confidential. Survey results were tallied, and first choices were weighted greater than second and third choices. Statistical numbers were not used; instead, the first three or four choices for desired training topics are shown in the results on page 39.

In addition, supervisors and their subordinates were asked to write answers to these two questions at the bottom of the survey:

1. What would help you become more effective in your position and advance your career goals?

2. What is the biggest threat to your success as a supervisor?

The answer to question 1 was often a request for training that had not been covered by the topics listed, or a desire for different field experience in order to be exposed to all aspects of the business.

The answer to question 2 yielded three types of answers:

• The supervisor was not threatened and felt that success would come over time with the appropriate development and experience.

• The supervisor had made a mistake(s) in the past and needed time to pass before another opportunity would arise to demonstrate growth and, ultimately, success.

• The supervisor felt like a "victim" and held others accountable for his or her lack of success. This is fairly typical for this type of survey. However, in one instance, 10 percent of the respondents said that since their organization was a closely held family-owned business, they felt advancement in their careers depended on being part of the family. No amount of training, development, or experience would advance their careers since promotions were given only to family members. This type of information did help the owners recognize that they were losing talented managers who thought they needed to change employers to advance their careers.

The tallied information and summary of narrative comments were shown to upper management so that training courses could be prioritized and sequenced.

# PRIORITIZE TRAINING NEEDS
## SAMPLE SUPERVISORY DEVELOPMENT ANALYSIS

*To All Supervisors: Rank first, second, and third the three courses that would be of greatest benefit to you and other supervisors at this company. Do this for each of three skill areas in each column. You will have six groupings of first, second, and third choices. Please read course descriptions before making choices.*

|  | You | All Other Supervisors |
|---|---|---|
| **PERSONAL SKILLS** (rank first, second, third) | | |
| Time Management | —— | —— |
| Active Listening | —— | —— |
| Problem Solving and Decision Making | —— | —— |
| Effective Presentations | —— | —— |
| Stress Management | —— | —— |
| Personal Computer Skills | —— | —— |
| **INTERPERSONAL SKILLS** (rank first, second, third) | | |
| Meeting Management | —— | —— |
| Business Writing | —— | —— |
| Team Building | —— | —— |
| Coaching and Counseling | —— | —— |
| Conflict Management | —— | —— |
| Motivation | —— | —— |
| Effective Communication | —— | —— |
| Dealing with Internal and External Customers | —— | —— |
| Self-Directed Work Teams | —— | —— |
| **SUPERVISION SKILLS** (rank first, second, third) | | |
| Managing Change | —— | —— |
| Delegation | —— | —— |
| Leadership and Empowerment | —— | —— |
| Progressive Discipline | —— | —— |
| Performance Appraisal | —— | —— |
| Selection Interviewing | —— | —— |
| Goal Setting | —— | —— |
| Training Subordinates | —— | —— |
| Labor Relations | —— | —— |

➤ What would help you become more effective and advance your career goals?


➤ What is the biggest threat to your success as a supervisor?

## Supervisory Development Survey Example

### Supervisory Narrative and Written Comments

The following is a summary of information collected from individual interviews of supervisors and from narrative comments on their written surveys. Twenty of the thirty target population supervisors were interviewed and completed a written survey. Thirty-five percent of the assembly workers also completed a written survey. The managers in this company up to this point had done only informal on-the-job training for the supervisors. Upper management became the feedback group to discuss and interpret the data.

### Comments from Supervisors

"It's pretty busy around here right now. I don't know if there is any time to attend a training class. You know, I've been at this job and in this business for over 25 years."

"I really have some trouble keeping the newer guys in line. If you give them an inch, they take a mile. I try to be patient, but if you don't kick them a little, the work never gets done. It seems that I need to be everywhere at one time."

"—— is really a good manager to work for. You going to tell him I said that? He could listen a bit more to our problems. There is just too much overtime right now. Everything is a rush. I go home tired; I wake up tired. It's not fun to come to work anymore, the way it used to be."

"The union is pretty good. But there are some guys that are always complaining about being singled out for discipline. I let them know right away what's wrong and how to fix it. Are we really going to have some training? That would be great. The other guys really need the help."

"How about not so much negative criticism? We occasionally hear about the good job we do, but there is never a comment on the small things. I've been in the same place for two years now. There is such pressure to catch up … all this over-time … my family just doesn't understand the pressure or the career opportunity that can come from it."

"I'd like to be able to spend more time with new people. There just never seems to be enough time to show them what's expected and how to do it right."

## Supervisory Development Survey Example

### Narrative Comments from the Supervisors' Subordinates

"It would really help my boss to listen before he climbs all over my case. I'd like some help from him instead of him always trying to write someone up. He thinks he's a real tough guy."

"I've seen an improvement in communication in the last month. That's the key to everything. We need more of that."

"Supervisors need to get more done through the foreman. Give each foreman an area to be responsible for instead of trying to do everything himself. This would free up your supervisors to make decisions, effect meaningful planning, and be more knowledgeable about all areas of the line."

"Supervisors need to have a more positive attitude. They are kind of suspicious most of the time. A little praise for a job well done would be appreciated."

"In the past, my supervisor has had a double standard. He's also not very good at listening."

"The supervisors are under constant and excessive pressure and lack of understanding from upper management about what really goes on down here."

"My supervisor lacks confidence. He changes his mind too easily."

"Maybe asking questions before jumping to conclusions about what has and has not been done, and who did it."

"More positive attitude toward labor relations."

"Act on employees' suggestions. Delegating more authority to us would create more harmony."

See a summary of the survey data below.

## Summary of Supervisors' Surveys

| Supervisors say "I need …" | Other supervisors need … | Workers say "supervisors need …" |
|---|---|---|
| **Personal Skills** | **Personal Skills** | **Personal Skills** |
| Time Management | Time Management | Problem Solving and Decision Making |
| Problem Solving and Decision Making | Active Listening | Active Listening |
| Stress Management | Problem Solving and Decision Making | Time Management |
| **Interpersonal Skills** | **Interpersonal Skills** | **Interpersonal Skills** |
| Coaching and Counseling | Team Building | Team Building |
| Motivation | Motivation | Effective Communication |
| Team Building | Coaching and Counseling | Motivation |
| Effective Communication | | Conflict Management |
| **Supervisory Skills** | **Supervisory Skills** | **Supervisory Skills** |
| Leadership Styles | Goal Setting | Leadership Styles |
| Training Subordinates | Leadership Styles | Labor Relations |
| Goal Setting | Training Subordinates | Delegation |

## Interpreting the Survey Results

Management had a large enough training budget to provide four one-day workshops. Take a few minutes to read the results and identify which four courses would provide the supervisors with the best development, keeping in mind that they have not had any previous training on any of these topics. Suggestions and conclusions about this type of survey follow.

## Decisions of the Management Group

1. Some topics were combined where appropriate in order to reduce expenses. For example, information about "Active Listening" was included in the class on "Effective Communication."

2. When the management group discussed the need for personal organizational skills, it was learned that there was a staffing shortage and once that was resolved, most believed the request for time management and stress management would disappear. "Problem Solving and Decision Making" and "Leadership Styles" were selected as two of the four courses based on their appearance on all three lists.

3. "Team Building" was not selected as an appropriate course, even though all three groups mentioned it. The narrative comments reveal that supervisors and subordinates had difficulty communicating. Providing that skill is a prerequisite to team building, which was deferred until after a foundation was created by the "Effective Communication" class.

4. Some of the training topics were named differently, depending on the perspective of the group. For example, supervisors say they want help in "Training Subordinates," while workers are asking for "Delegation" training for the supervisors. The management group concluded that the reason supervisors weren't delegating was because of the low level of skill in their subordinates. Likewise, the supervisors' request for "Goal Setting" training was described by the workers as a request for "Labor Relations." In this unionized environment, supervisors were eager to set aggressive work standards and goals. Workers wanted their supervisors to abide by what had been agreed to through negotiations.

5. The fourth class was a combination of Motivation, Coaching, Counseling, and Discipline. As the other three classes progressed, it became more obvious that the problems the supervisors faced often involved dealing with subordinates in a positive manner.

6. The following sequence of the four workshops was initially agreed upon:

   — Leadership Styles

   — Effective Communication

   — Problem Solving and Decision Making

   — Motivation, Coaching, Counseling, and Discipline

At the end of the second class, the supervisors were asked to identify two or three typical problems they wanted the class to work on during the next workshop. Since most of the problems involved Motivation, Coaching, Counseling, and Discipline, that class was resequenced as the third class, and Problem Solving became the final workshop.

In summary, the development needs of the supervisors were prioritized and confirmed when more than one group identified that need. The decision to conduct a particular workshop was tied to a business need when the management discussed the data and interpreted the remarks of those who were interviewed. This organization reduced training expenses by prioritizing training needs and conducting training in a sequence that benefited the greatest number of supervisors.

## PRIORITIZE TRAINING
## DECISION CHECKLIST

*Consider these items when deciding how to use information from the needs vs. wants survey:*

_____ 1. Can topics be combined or renamed to provide appropriate training?

_____ 2. Which topics demonstrate strong interest and are identified by more than one group?

_____ 3. Does the selected course(s) address a root cause of poor performance and not a symptom or a desire?

_____ 4. Use narrative comments to prove selection by topic.

_____ 5. Are classes sequenced so prerequisite skills are met?

_____ 6. Do different groups identify the same issue by different names because of different points of view?

_____ 7. Be willing to change the courses selected as additional information becomes available.

_____ 8. Be willing to resequence courses as needed.

_____ 9. Are courses selected related to a business need?

_____ 10. Do you have consensus on the needs to be met by conducting training?

So far, two tools to assess needs have been provided: performance analysis and prioritizing training needs analysis. Performance analysis helps the training professional decide if training is an appropriate solution to a performance problem. The prioritizing training needs analysis helps the training professional select training that is tied to a business need and is a confirmed need, rather than the desire of a limited number of employees to increase skills.

Two additional types of needs analysis that can help the trainer clarify training needs are Goal Analysis and Target Population Analysis. Goal Analysis is a consensus process of making a vague desire specific. Target Population Analysis identifies who would benefit from the training and how the training can be customized.

# Goal Analysis

## Purpose

The purpose of Goal Analysis is to make a vague desire specific and measurable through a consensus process.

## When to Use Goal Analysis

The training professional can use Goal Analysis for one of two purposes:

1. In response to requests for improved performance that are originally described in vague or attitudinal terms. For example, a training goal may be described as "Let's make our sales people more professional," or "Let's encourage our customer service reps to be more empathetic and understanding," or "Let's have our analysts work smarter, not harder."

2. To develop specific objectives from a broader human resources plan or operational plan (one-year or five-year plan, etc.)

## How to Conduct Goal Analysis

The process of goal analysis can be formal or informal, depending on the purpose and amount of time available to determine the goal of the requested training. If a colleague makes an informal comment about "making our sales people more professional," it may not warrant a formal investigation. However, if the Sales Manager describes a number of complaints and an amount of lost sales, a more formal investigation could be appropriate.

**INFORMAL APPROACH**

Question the colleague and ask him or her to describe specific behaviors that would make the sales people more professional. Identify which behaviors are missing and whether training has any role in improving sales.

**FORMAL APPROACH**

1. Conduct a written survey of individuals who are aware of the need to reach a particular goal and could be helpful in describing the goal more specifically. It may be helpful to have a list of adjectives for survey respondents to identify as appropriate characteristics of those who might need training.

2. Ask a representative group to meet as a task force and more specifically describe the goal. Ask the group to reach consensus about what needs to be done to reach the specifically described goal.

## Dimensions for Consensus Discussion

To create a goal statement, use these steps:

1. Create an initial *written* statement that specifies and summarizes the desired outcome. Using the five-part SMART goal process can be helpful. SMART stands for:

   — S = specific behavior (what can be seen or heard?)

   — M = measurable behavior (how will success be determined?)

   — A = achievable goal (what behavior can be reached?)

   — R = realistic behavior (what is possible for this person in this environment?)

   — T = time bound (when will the goal be reached?)

2. Prioritize the list of behaviors or performances through consensus discussion.

3. Rewrite the initial goal statement using the prioritized list of behaviors. A possible format could be, "If our sales people (insert name of target population) were to become more professional (insert desired behavior or attitude), they would do the following … (list performances).

4. Test the written statement by asking several knowledgeable parties if the target group were to do the specifically described behaviors, would they be considered (insert goal) professional, more empathetic, etc.

In summary, by using goal analysis, the training professional can clarify exactly what behaviors need training and provide only the specific training that will meet the expectations of managers and others requesting training.

# GOAL ANALYSIS CHECKLIST

*Consider these issues when conducting a goal analysis:*

_____ 1. Is the goal stated in vague or attitudinal terms, and does it need to be made more specific?

_____ 2. Is the goal stated for a specific training event or for a larger plan over a period of time?

_____ 3. Can the goal analysis be done quickly and informally by questioning the person requesting the training event?

_____ 4. Write questions to ask the person requesting the training event to make the outcome more specific.

_____ 5. Is a survey appropriate to identify specific characteristics needed to reach the goal?

_____ 6. Do you need a task force to assist in describing the goal in specific terms?

_____ 7. Write a goal statement using the five-part SMART process.

_____ 8. Prioritize the list of behaviors or performances during a consensus discussion.

_____ 9. Rewrite the goal statement using the prioritized list of behaviors.

_____ 10. Test the written goal statement with knowledgeable parties to be sure it is complete and meets a business need.

# Target Population Analysis

## Purpose

Target population analysis helps the training professional decide who needs training, how to customize a specific course to meet the participants' needs, and what class groupings are appropriate.

## Analysis Steps

Collect information from at least three of the six categories below. All categories do not have equal importance for each training event. Decide what information about this group can help make enrollment and grouping decisions. Information is best collected from interviews and observations since written surveys frequently raise suspicions. Work records and other existing reports can sometimes provide good data if viewing them does not violate employee confidentiality.

## Categories of Information

1. *Interests.* What avocations, personal or business interests or current events are important to the target population? This information can be used to customize examples and exercises that relate to what is already known.

2. *Prior training.* Don't bore someone with repeated information. Knowing prior training will assist in: 1) grouping, 2) setting prerequisite requirements and 3) other administrative decisions.

3. *Personal benefit to learning.* What personal or professional rewards does the trainee gain from the class? Keys to motivation may influence opening exercises and the need to develop supervisory support and follow-up for this training program. The WIIMF factor—"What's in it for me?"—often plays a role in the level of participants' motivation.

4. *Attitudes and biases.* Attitudes may be analyzed as follows.

   — What is the attitude toward one's job? Is work defined as something you get paid for, doing what one is trained to do, or is the larger purpose of an employee's work evident?

   — What is the attitude toward learning in general? Do participants believe something new can be learned all the time, or did meaningful learning end with formal schooling?

   — What is the attitude of most participants toward this specific class? Is it mandated by law or company dictate? Is the class's reputation favorable or unfavorable? Attitudes and biases dramatically influence selection of content, grouping, and supervisory follow-up.

5. *Physical characteristics.* The age, sex, and physical dexterity of the target population could influence content selection, amount of practice required to learn a skill, etc. For example, it may take a person who is petite more time to learn a skill such as Cardiopulmonary Resuscitation (CPR). The more homogeneous

the group, the easier it becomes to streamline the content and process of instruction.

6. *Cultural characteristics.* Identify the reading level of nonnative English-speaking learners. The content and amount of material covered may need to be altered, or other accommodations can be made. For example, if key words must be used, provide a glossary of key terms or translate them into the learner's native language. Become familiar enough with cultural taboos so that organization norms are not violated by the content and process of instruction.

## Summarize the Information

Once the appropriate information from the six categories above is developed, write a narrative statement about the group that describes who will attend the planned training. Test the statement by sharing it with others who have knowledge of this group. Ask what other information needs to be included about the group to make decisions about the training. Finally, if further information needs to be developed, what sources are available to provide the information?

# TARGET POPULATION ANALYSIS
# DECISION CHECKLIST

*Use the target population statement you have developed to make several decisions:*

1. Remind the course developer who the typical learner is and suggest examples that might be appropriate for this group.

2. Discuss with the course developer the time constraints and how much practice is required to learn the skills and meet the course objectives for this training.

3. Identify how many people are included in this target population.

4. Identify how many groupings will be needed to completely train this group.

5. Identify any prerequisites that need to be met for this training. Share these expectations and requirements with the supervisor of these employees.

6. Does the course developer need to create special examples or materials to meet the needs subgroups of employees who will be trained.

7. Is it realistic to train all the employees in a specific group at the same time? Is it necessary to schedule part of the population to attend training while other employees keep the work going?

8. Can different levels of employees be trained in the same group? Is it appropriate or threatening if supervisors are trained in the same group with their subordinates?

9. To make the training as cost effective as possible, who is a secondary target audience who can benefit from this training? What would be the additional cost to train this additional group? What is the benefit to these employees and the organization to attend training that is not specifically targeted to them?

10. What are the benefits of attending this training? How can this information and information about attitudes and biases for this training be used to make appealing training announcements?

## Final Assessment Suggestions

Additional resources for conducting a performance analysis, goal analysis, and target analysis are included in the bibliography.

Once information from these four types of assessments is developed, a training plan should be drawn up using this information. This training plan should address training needs that are to be met over a period of time and take between one to five years to implement.

## Benefits of Planning

Planning for training allows the organization to

- Anticipate and meet business development needs

- Anticipate and meet business maintenance needs

- Anticipate staffing needs

- Use resources wisely

- Avoid problems that often arise without planning

Planning for training allows the trainer to

- Schedule training to meet the development needs of the operation

- Anticipate the need for course development and delivery

- Identify appropriate resources to develop and deliver the training

- Conserve training resources by ensuring that training events are tied to a business need

- Prioritize activities to meet shared expectations and reach a planned outcome

## Training Plan Overview

Usually, a training plan is written to meet projected training needs for a group of employees (e.g., first line supervisors) for a specific development need (e.g., how to complete a performance review), for a period of time (the coming year). Useful training plans have ten parts, which are described in the following sections.

### 1. Define the Business Issue:

Define the issues related to a business need that training can address. Not all business needs are appropriately addressed by training. Performance analysis (shown in Chapter 3) can identify appropriate training issues. For example, for either of the following issues it would be appropriate to develop a training plan:

- How can we develop assistant store managers so they can successfully open ten new stores when they are promoted to store manager in the next 12 months?

- Middle managers have no advanced training beyond what they received when they became supervisors. Middle managers complete performance appraisals subjectively, show favoritism to certain subordinates and have grievances filed against them.

## 2. Distinguish Training Needs vs. Training Wants:

Some organizations get trapped into offering training programs because they are popular or requested, without regard for need. Often a request for "time management," "stress management," or "communication skills" indicates "needs" that should be differentiated from "wants." Use the Prioritize Training Needs Sample Supervisory Development Analysis (page 37) to identify whether such a request is related to job performance.

## 3. Establish a Partnership with Supervisors:

How will managers or supervisors of those attending training be included in the planning and follow-up for improved performance? The partnership model in Chapter 2 shows how to share roles and responsibilities to make the training successful.

## 4. Identify or Establish Performance Standards:

Training is often requested to improve performance. Is there a performance standard to use as the goal for a minimum level of acceptable performance? The operational area, not training, needs to establish job performance standards. It becomes difficult to train if vague or no standards exist. Make vague desires more specific through Goal Analysis. Instead of trying to meet a request to "just make them more professional," Goal Analysis helps establish a standard of acceptable job performance.

## 5. Identify the Trainees:

Who will be trained? What job classifications do they hold, and how many people need training? Conduct a Target Population Analysis and include a recommendation for the decisions listed on page 48 as part of the training plan.

## 6. Establish Training Objectives:

What are the learning objectives for the training program? What skills is the target population expected to acquire by attending the training. Identify how learning objectives will be measured. Chapter 15 contains information about how to evaluate learning.

## 7. Cost of Training:

What are the costs involved in assessing the need for training, designing the training, developing or buying learner and instructor materials, presenting the training, and evaluating the training? Are the costs worth the benefit? If upper management is reluctant to allocate resources to train employees, it may be appropriate to identify the operational costs of not doing any training. For example, what is the level of grievances based on current performance and what is that costing the operation?

## 8. Select and Develop the Training Program:

Will you select the training program from an outside vendor or develop the training program internally? Various options include

- Delivering an existing program using internal subject matter experts.

- Developing a training program using internal subject matter experts.

- Buying a package program and using internal subject matter experts to deliver the training.

- Hiring an external consultant or vendor to design and deliver the training.

## 9. Schedule the Training:

What time of the day, week, month, quarter, or year is best for this type of training? What are the consequences of training "on the clock" vs. on the employee's own time in your organization? Additional information about scheduling training can be found in Chapter 11.

## 10. Evaluate the Results:

How will you know whether the training is successful? How will learning and new skills be evaluated? How will you tie training to bottom line results? For example, have grievances been reduced? Chapter 15 discusses how to evaluate training.

# TRAINING PLAN
# TEMPLATE CHECKLIST

*Use this checklist to identify whether all parts of a training plan are complete.*

\_\_\_\_\_ 1. Clearly define a business issue that can be addressed through training.

\_\_\_\_\_ 2. Distinguish training needs vs. training wants. What is the skill that is missing that can be addressed through training?

\_\_\_\_\_ 3. Establish a partnership with supervisors. What are the shared roles for training and management?

\_\_\_\_\_ 4. Identify performance standards or establish standards if none exist.

\_\_\_\_\_ 5. Identify trainees. Who would benefit from training? What is the primary audience? Is there a secondary audience that could also benefit from the training?

\_\_\_\_\_ 6. Establish training objectives. What will the target population be able to do as a result of the training?

\_\_\_\_\_ 7. Estimate cost of training. Also, estimate the potential cost if no training is done.

\_\_\_\_\_ 8. Select and develop the training program. Which option seems most reasonable?

- Delivering an existing program using internal subject matter experts

- Developing a training program using internal subject matter experts

- Buying a packaged program and using internal subject matter experts to deliver the training

- Hiring an external consultant or vendor to design and deliver the training

\_\_\_\_\_ 9. Schedule according to business demands. When could most of the target population attend this training?

\_\_\_\_\_ 10. Evaluate the results. Estimate the cost savings and how that will be measured following training.

Chapter 4

# How to Select Training Programs and Packages Employees Want to Use

## Objectives

- How to select the best resource to provide training.

- How to buy external training programs.

- How to participate in buying decisions.

- Set objectives for training events.

- Establish requirements to buy packaged training programs and training videos—what does good training look like?

- Identify external resources for training programs.

- Identify criteria to review external training proposals.

## Chapter Tools

- How to Buy Package Program Checklist

- Selecting Package Training Program Checklist

- Select the Best Resources Template

## Questions

Answer this question to identify the development level for the issues addressed in this chapter.

1. *How are packaged training programs selected?*

    — Stage 1: There are no clear criteria for the selection of training packages.

    — Stage 2: Selection criteria are clear. Proposals are requested to compare similar packages. References are checked.

    — Stage 3: Packaged training programs are reviewed as needed with input from internal clients and measured against criteria.

    — Stage 4: A systematic process exists for gathering resources, reviewing and selecting training packages with input from internal clients, and measuring them against criteria.

    — Stage 5: In addition to accomplishing what is done in Stage 4, each request for a new program is matched to the changing needs of the organization.

If you rated yourself at Stage 1 or Stage 2 for this diagnostic question, you might want to proceed through this chapter as it is written. If you rated yourself at Stage 3 or higher, you might benefit from previewing the tools provided in this chapter before working through the ideas and suggestions provided with the checklists.

## The Buying Process

In order to meet business needs, the trainer should plan the buying process instead of buying impulsively when considering training programs, training packages, and training videos. Analyzing the need for training and developing criteria to describe effective training will enable you to achieve better results. To select the best resources, use the checklist on the following page that describes a 15-step method to help simplify the buying process.

You will have more opportunities to participate in a buying decision if you can convince management that you are using a well-thought-out process.

# HOW TO BUY PACKAGE
# PROGRAM CHECKLIST

*Use the following questions as a checklist when planning to buy outside resources for training.*

_____  1. What is the clearly established business need?

_____  2. Is the training request important?

_____  3. Is there a skill deficiency and therefore a training need?

_____  4. Who needs training and how many people need training?

_____  5. Have written training objectives been developed that are specific, measurable, and attainable?

_____  6. What content would meet these objectives?

_____  7. How much training is needed (how long will the training take)?

_____  8. Is there a job standard or expected proficiency level requirement?

_____  9. How will you know whether you are successful (what is the means to measure the success of the training)?

_____  10. What resources are currently available internally?

_____  11. What is the best method of delivery of training (self-paced, classroom, OJT, CBT, etc.)?

_____  12. Have you developed a "statement of work" listing your objectives along with the needs to be filled by an external resource?

_____  13. Have you developed a list of qualified outside resources?

_____  14. Have you developed criteria to evaluate written proposals from outside resources?

_____  15. Have you developed a realistic time line for this project?

### Set the Objective

Before buying a training program, identify the objective that will be met by purchasing it. If you are not armed with a clear objective, vendors can easily persuade you that their package is the best.

What is the reason behind a request for training? The need for training can be assessed using one or more of the four assessment tools described in Chapter 3. Once the business need is verified, identify the appropriate learning objective for the target audience. Sample business needs and learning objectives are matched to sample training programs in the table below. When reviewing or screening potential programs or packages, identify whether the contents of the training package will meet the learning objectives.

Also, identify the type of learning objective the package intends to meet. Is the training package aimed at providing information and acquiring new skill as well as knowledge? In the two examples below, the learners need to acquire new information and additional skills if they are to meet a business need. If the objective is to build a skill, the training program needs to provide an opportunity for employees to practice using the skill. Training programs or packages or videos that do not provide skill practice would not be appropriate to meet the business needs in the examples below. If the training package is constructed around a video, are discussion questions and facilitation directions provided as part of the training package?

| Business Need | Learning Objective | Training Package Contains |
|---|---|---|
| Retail store managers are experiencing a high turnover rate for new clerks during the first 30 days of employment. | By the end of the training, the store managers will be able to conduct a selection interview that screens out poor job candidates. | • How to ask screening questions<br>• How to avoid asking illegal questions |
| Supervisors are not writing disciplinary notices for employees who underperform or act inappropriately. | By the end of the training, the supervisor will write an appropriately worded disciplinary notice. | • Situations that violate company policy<br>• How to counsel subordinates<br>• How to write a disciplinary notice |

### Identify External Resources

To identify appropriate external resources, use some or all of the following leads:

- Ask professional associations if they have a directory of services. (See the list of professional associations in Appendix B.)

- Ask your friends, and network with other training professionals who might have a resource that would be appropriate.

- Search the World Wide Web. Suggested Web sites are listed in Appendix B.

- Search the business section of the public library for business directories. The business reference librarian can offer suggestions to locate resources.

## Set Criteria to Review Training Proposals

The checklist on the following page suggests points to judge for resources under review. You should decide whether the objective of the program matches your objective. Does the material include your industry in its examples, or do the examples need to be customized before presenting this training? What is the quality of the content of the material? Is it thorough or superficial? If the objective is to acquire skill, is the amount of skill practice appropriate and realistic for your organization? How does the material compare with others in the same price range? Is the material a good value for the cost and a reasonable answer to the business need? And finally, what is your recommendation for this product or program?

Once several resources are compared against the criteria, then they can be measured against each other to determine which product, program, or video provides the greatest value for the investment while meeting your objectives. It may not be possible to find a training product, program, or video that meets all your criteria and objectives; therefore, it may be helpful to prioritize the criteria and establish a point system that assigns a value to measure the extent to which criteria are met. The Select the Best Resources template on page 59 will help you make selection decisions.

# SELECTING PACKAGE TRAINING PROGRAM CHECKLIST

Date: _____

Title: _____ Class Length: _____

Vendor: _____ Reviewer's Name: _____

| Check the appropriate column | good | poor |
|---|---|---|
| Clearly stated objective | ____ | ____ |
| Objective matches your program objective | ____ | ____ |

Material fits your industry
- Only for your industry       ____     ____
- General enough/willing to customize     ____     ____

Content
- Comprehensive and inclusive      ____     ____
- Too much covered/too little       ____     ____
- Knowledge and concepts are clear    ____     ____
- Examples specific and concrete      ____     ____
- Examples realistic and believable     ____     ____
- Skill practice appropriate

Technical quality of
- Video                   ____     ____
- Leader's guide          ____     ____
- Handouts, workbooks      ____     ____
- Visuals/transparencies     ____     ____

Opportunity for follow-up presented    ____     ____

Cost: ____ buy/license, ____ rent, ____ preview

General Comments:

_____

Overall rating                       ____     ____

Recommend: ____ buy/license, ____ rent, ____ reject

# SELECT THE BEST RESOURCES TEMPLATE

Award points to each product using the following criteria:

Name of reviewer: _____ Date: _____

| Suggested Criteria | Product #1 | Product #2 | Product #3 |
|---|---|---|---|
| Clearly stated objective | | | |
| Objectives match my objectives | | | |
| Materials need to be customized | | | |
| Materials match or fit our industry | | | |
| Comprehensive content | | | |
| Content clearly presented | | | |
| Examples clear and concrete | | | |
| Examples realistic and believable | | | |
| Appropriate skill practice | | | |
| Technical quality of video | | | |
| Technical quality of leader's guide | | | |
| Technical quality of workbook or handout | | | |
| Cost is reasonable value | | | |
| Other factors: | | | |
| | | | |
| | | | |
| Total Points | | | |

Recommendation:

Chapter 5

# How to Select and Coach Subject Matter Experts as Internal Trainers

## Objectives

- Use internal subject matter experts (SMEs) as trainers.

- Establish a process to select subject matter experts as internal trainers.

- Use a process to support, develop, coach, and give feedback to internal trainers.

## Chapter Tools

- Qualifications for Internal Trainers

- Internal Trainer Selection Process Checklist

- Sample Letter of Invitation to Internal Trainer Candidates

- Internal Trainer Agreement

- Feedback and Coaching Template for Internal Trainers

## Questions

Answer these four questions to identify your current development level for the issues addressed in this chapter.

1. *Which stage of development describes how subject matter experts are selected as internal trainers?*

   — Stage 1: No clear criteria exist for the selection of subject matter experts as internal trainers.

   — Stage 2: Selection criteria for subject matter experts as internal trainers are clear. Trainers usually have high subject matter expertise and recent field experience.

   — Stage 3: Written requirements for subject matter experts as internal trainers cover knowledge of subject matter, training skills, and practical expertise in the field.

   — Stage 4: A formal assessment process has subject matter experts demonstrate knowledge, training skills, and practical expertise in the field.

   — Stage 5: In addition to Stage 4, subject matter experts have demonstrated ability to relate learning and training to organizational business needs.

2. *Which stage of development describes how internal trainers get feedback?*

   — Stage 1: Internal trainers receive no formal feedback, although some may solicit informal feedback from learners.

   — Stage 2: Feedback is received randomly and only occasionally from the line supervisor or trainer. Some feedback is provided by written participant end-of-course evaluations.

   — Stage 3: Internal trainers get regular feedback from the line supervisor, the trainer, and participants' evaluations.

   — Stage 4: Internal trainer competencies are regularly assessed through end-of-course evaluations and visits by on-site trainers and/or line supervisors. Training skills are assessed during performance appraisals.

   — Stage 5: Feedback and trend analysis are used extensively.

3. *Which stage of development describes how internal trainers improve their skills?*

   — Stage 1: Internal trainers received no train-the-trainer skill development.

   — Stage 2: Internal trainers develop training skills on their own.

   — Stage 3: Internal trainers are encouraged to attend outside train-the-trainer courses. An occasional in-house train-the-trainer course may be offered.

   — Stage 4: Internal trainers receive systematic development by practical experience in their subject area. Most SMEs share time between training and other duties.

   — Stage 5: Internal trainers get knowledge, practical training, and field experience for continuous improvement.

4. Which stage of development describes methodologies used by internal trainers?

— Stage 1: Internal trainers' methods are limited to lecture, large group discussion, demonstration, and practice sessions.

— Stage 2: Internal trainers' methods include adult learning techniques.

— Stage 3: Internal trainers' methods include appropriate participation, pacing, and discovery learning.

— Stage 4: Internal trainers use a variety of training methods to enhance the effectiveness of training.

— Stage 5: Internal trainers use state-of-the-art methods to help meet the business need through training.

If you rated yourself at Stage 1 or Stage 2 for most of these diagnostic questions, you might want to proceed through this chapter as it is written. If you rated yourself at Stage 3 or higher, you might benefit from previewing the tools provided in this chapter before working through the ideas and suggestions provided with the checklists.

## Select Subject Matter Experts as Internal Trainers

Employees with subject matter expertise are good candidates to become trainers because they are well regarded by their peers and have a strong foundation of practical knowledge and skills, which they can use effectively to develop the skills of other employees. SMEs must be available for a training assignment and willing to spend part of their time planning and conducting training sessions. This chapter offers practical suggestions for how to select SMEs as internal trainers, how to provide feedback to develop SMEs, and how to develop training skills in SMEs so they can use adult learning methods and achieve the expected results.

### How to Select Subject Matter Experts As Internal Trainers

After considering the general selection criteria, each organization needs to identify additional appropriate criteria to select subject matter experts for training duties. The checklist on the following page suggests qualifications for subject matter experts to become internal trainers.

# QUALIFICATIONS FOR INTERNAL TRAINERS

*Ask the subject matter expert to rate him/herself on the following areas of expertise.*

Use the following scale to identify each requirement:

0 = does not meet the requirement

1 = meets the requirement at a minimal level

2 = meets the requirement beyond the minimal level

The subject matter expert has:

_____ Time available for a training assignment

_____ Willingness to take on training assignments

_____ Specific knowledge needed by others

_____ Practical experience in completing tasks that meet the job standard

_____ Experience in conducting classroom training or giving presentations

_____ Experience in coaching or mentoring others

_____ Experience conducting one-on-one training or on-the-job training

_____ Good verbal communication skills

_____ Good written communication skills

_____ Facilitated team meetings or has been a team leader

_____ Total score

Interpretation

A perfect score is 20. Since a candidate who scores less than 12 points has minimal skills in some important requirements, this SME may not be the best candidate to train others in your organization. Also, the SME who does not have time or is unwilling to take on a training assignment may not be a good internal trainer candidate.

## Internal Trainer Selection Process

First, decide how formal or informal the selection process will be. If subject matter experts are to become full-time internal trainers and have a change in job assignment, then a formal selection process may be appropriate. If subject matter experts will have part-time training responsibilities while maintaining their current job duties, then a less formal selection process may work. So, the first decision is whether the internal trainer assignment is full-time or part-time. The second decision is whether the assignment is temporary or permanent. Will the SME identify this assignment as an upward step in a career path and therefore a benefit? If this assignment is an upward step, there may be a greater number of SMEs who will want to be considered. When the SME has finished a job rotation as a trainer, will a comparable and desirable job be available in the operation?

See the Internal Trainer Selection Process Checklist on the next page for additional steps in the process. To gain the greatest participation and select the best candidates, send an open invitation to potential candidates or use your organization's job-posting process. Identify the benefits of the position and the duties and responsibilities as well as the training and support that will be provided to develop SMEs as internal trainers. See the sample letter of invitation on page 67. To formalize the internal trainer assignment, complete a letter of agreement between the internal trainer candidate and that employee's supervisor. See the sample agreement on page 68.

To maintain the internal trainer's skills, create a feedback and coaching process for continued development and as a means of identifying potential problems. See the Feedback and Coaching Template for Internal Trainers on page 69. To use this form, rate the trainer's performance by identifying what is positive and interesting, and give suggestions for what the trainer can do to improve performance next time. Use this form to review three types of training skills: content, process, and use of adult learning steps. Ask the trainer in what area of development he or she would like feedback. Peers and class participants can also help evaluate a trainer. After the class session, ask trainers to comment on their strengths and anything "interesting" that they might have been trying out for the first time. Also ask trainers to explain what they might do differently next time. Then ask other observers for their comments, and, finally, offer your own comments and suggestions. An explanation of what to include in the five steps of adult learning can be found in Appendix C.

# INTERNAL TRAINER SELECTION
# PROCESS CHECKLIST

*Use this form to make critical decisions to set up a process to select subject matter experts as internal trainers. This form might best be used in a consensus decision process by various stakeholders in the organization and the training function.*

_____ 1. Determine whether the assignment as an Internal Trainer is a full-time or part-time responsibility?

_____ 2. Determine whether the assignment is temporary or permanent?

_____ 3. Select criteria to qualify internal trainer candidates.

_____ 4. Send an invitation to qualified candidates or post job openings using normal procedures.

_____ 5. Create an Internal Trainer Agreement that describes duties, responsibilities and support to develop the SME as an internal trainer.

_____ 6. Provide a train-the-trainer workshop to help SMEs gain adult learning or teaching skills and become familiar with the content of the material they will teach.

_____ 7. Set up a feedback and coaching process as support for the internal trainers.

_____ 8. How will internal trainers be evaluated and rewarded?

_____ 9. How will you maintain and develop internal trainers for those who transition to a full-time or permanent assignment?

_____ 10. Provide materials and audiovisual support to the SMEs.

# SAMPLE LETTER OF INVITATION TO
# INTERNAL TRAINER CANDIDATES

[date]

[first and last name]

[title]

[address]

Dear [first name],

Because of your knowledge, skill, and experience, you are being considered for a [full/part] time position as an internal trainer. Materials [have/have not] been prepared to teach [insert course title] and we are seeking individuals who meet many of the qualifications in the attached checklist. Please rate yourself on the checklist and ask your manager to rate you as well to determine your qualifications for this assignment.

We are going to conduct a train-the-trainer workshop for qualified internal trainer candidates on [insert date, time and place] to help candidates learn the content of the workshop and how to teach the material.

We hope you will review the attached Internal Trainer Agreement and Qualifications and discuss them with your supervisor. Let us know of your willingness to participate in this assignment by returning the completed Internal Trainer Agreement to my office by [date]. I hope you will join us in this effort to [state business need]. If you have questions, you can reach me at [insert telephone/e-mail].

Sincerely,



[name]

[title]

Enclosures

# INTERNAL TRAINER AGREEMENT

*Use this sample agreement to formalize job responsibilities of subject matter experts as internal trainers. As with any agreement, your organization's legal counsel should review this form for compliance with your policies and procedures.*

Name _____     Title _____

Department _____     E-mail _____

Phone _____     Fax _____

Mailing address _____

This agreement to serve as a certified trainer is a shared responsibility for the trainer and his or her supervisor. The duties and time commitment agreement must be signed by both the trainer and his/her supervisor.

The trainer agrees to:

- Complete a trainer certification process that involves attending a two-day train-the-trainer workshop and a one-day practice session and co-teaching the one-day class.

- The trainer agrees to be available for 24 months from the date of signature to teach _____ workshop(s) for up to 15 days per year.

- The trainer agrees to teach the workshop using the stated objectives and content.

- The trainer agrees to an evaluation every six months and to take steps to improve performance as a trainer if needed.

_____     _____
Trainer's signature                 Date

I will support _____ in serving as a trainer by allowing him/her time to prepare for and conduct this one-day workshop.

_____     _____
Supervisor's signature              Date

# FEEDBACK AND COACHING TEMPLATE
# FOR INTERNAL TRAINERS

Topic: _____ Facilitator: _____

Observer's name: _____

Use these letters in the space at the left below to rate my observation:

**P** = positive aspect of this presentation
**I** = interesting aspect of this presentation
**N** = I suggest a different approach for next time**

CONTENT OBSERVATION:

_____ Information given is accurate

_____ Shared what was to be learned (objective) and why (WIIFM)

_____ Session starter meets criteria: low risk, everyone participated, relevant

_____ Enough examples were given to promote understanding

_____ Worded questions appropriately

_____ Summary/application appropriate

PROCESS OBSERVATION:

_____ Participants active 50 percent of the time

_____ Used a variety of learning methods and techniques

_____ Managed anxiety well in front of the group

_____ Gave clear directions

_____ Used overhead projector or easel pad appropriately

_____ Used time well (not rushed or too slow)

STEPS OF ADULT LEARNING OBSERVATION:

_____ Set up the activity

_____ Conduct the activity

_____ Share and interpret reactions

_____ Identify concepts

_____ Apply concepts to their situations

Comments on strengths of this presenter:


Suggestions for next time:

Chapter 6

# How to Keep Training Courses Up to Date

## Objectives

- Establish who maintains courses.
- Establish how to maintain courses.
- Establish what a good leader's guide looks like.
- Establish multiple roles for trainers.

## Chapter Tools

- Course Maintenance Checklist, Part 1
- Course Maintenance Checklist, Part 2
- Guide to Select Types of Lesson Plans
- Develop Lesson Plans Checklist

## Questions

Answer these four questions to identify your current development level for the issues addressed in this chapter.

1. *Which stage of development describes how courses are maintained?*

   — Stage 1: No systematic maintenance of courses exists. Trainers often use technical manuals in place of handout materials.

   — Stage 2: One subject matter expert or trainer becomes responsible for course maintenance of a purchased course. Internal course refinements imitate the external vendor's methods.

   — Stage 3: Key subject matter experts (SMEs) trainers are responsible for course maintenance with occasional input from others.

   — Stage 4: Key SMEs are responsible for course maintenance and systematically ask for input from others.

   — Stage 5: Key SMEs are responsible for course maintenance through research, trend analysis and input from other SMEs and internal customers.

2. *Which stage of development describes leader and facilitator guides used by internal trainers?*

   — Stage 1: No lesson plan or facilitator guide exists.

   — Stage 2: A leader's guide is provided by external vendors.

   — Stage 3: Leader's guides are developed internally in an outline format.

   — Stage 4: Leader's guides are developed internally, and format is based on assessment of the course and the instructor's needs.

   — Stage 5: Leader's guides are developed and improved internally based on an ongoing assessment and feedback from users.

3. *Which stage of development describes the multiple roles of internal trainers?*

   — Stage 1: Technical trainers complete testing and certification to present subject in their expertise.

   — Stage 2: Internal trainers are divided into two groups: those who instruct and those who instruct and update courses.

   — Stage 3: Trainers are cross-trained to present multiple programs. All trainers provide input on course revisions. External trainers are limited to new course development beyond internal expertise.

   — Stage 4: Key trainers systematically identify business needs and the effects of training.

   — Stage 5: Training needs are aligned with business needs and courses are evaluated for bottom line results. Results are routinely reported to management.

If you rated yourself at Stage 1 or Stage 2 for most of these diagnostic questions, you might want to proceed through this chapter as it is written. If you rated yourself at Stage 3 or higher, you might benefit from previewing the tools provided in this chapter before working through the ideas and suggestions provided with the checklists.

## Systematic Course Maintenance

Once a training course is purchased or developed, it often needs to be adapted in order to keep the course current and still meet the needs of the employees and the organization. If no system exists to keep track of course maintenance, the trainer might teach an outdated procedure, process, or policy and end up confusing employees instead of providing new skills. Course maintenance will be performed more frequently if a specific individual is given the responsibility to keep the course up to date. Input and suggestions to keep a course up to date should come from the following sources:

- The trainer

- The participants

- The operational or internal customer

- External customers

See the two-part checklist on the following pages to identify how to set up a course maintenance process.

One of the key sources of information for suggested course updates is provided by the feedback sheets or end-of-course reaction sheets completed by the participants. A sample reaction sheet is shown in Chapter 15.

# COURSE MAINTENANCE CHECKLIST, PART 1

Name of course  _____

Date purchased _____ Date first presented  _____

Vendor or course developer  _____

Developer contact information  _____

Describe the need that led to the development or purchase of this course:

_____

What customization (if any) was done when the course was developed to meet this need?  _____

_____

List the dates when this course was conducted during the last year:  _____

_____

How many employees have attended this course in the past year?  _____

Name of employee or trainer responsible for updates:  _____

Describe the changes made to the course beyond clerical updates:

_____

_____

_____

_____

Have feedback sheets been reviewed for information about course updates and/or improvements?

Which of the following have been consulted for course improvements?

_____ internal trainers/SMEs

_____ external trainers

_____ course participants

_____ supervisors of course participants

_____ others

# COURSE MAINTENANCE CHECKLIST, PART 2

On at least an annual basis, review the following for improvement:

## Course Content

_____ Are policies up to date?

_____ Are procedures up to date?

_____ Are processes up to date?

_____ Is new technical information available from internal or external sources that could suggest changes to the examples in the course materials?

_____ Is the layout and graphic appearance of the participant materials appropriate?

## Audiovisuals and Job Aids

_____ Are changes necessary in these materials to reflect changes to the course content?

_____ Are additional job aids requested by participants or their supervisors to help transfer of learning to the job?

_____ Is new technology available that can enhance learning that may not have been available when the course was developed?

## Leader's Guide

_____ Are changes necessary to reflect changes in the course materials?

_____ Have the instructors requested additional background or resources in order to provide a better understanding of course content?

_____ Have the instructors requested additional information about how to tie specific information to course objectives?

_____ Have instructors requested additional information about how to provide answers to typical participant questions?

_____ Have instructors requested additional information about the process of learning?

## Lesson Plan Development

Developing an appropriate lesson plan for a course can make the difference between a failed and a successful presentation of a course. There are three formats for lesson plans: overview, outline, and scripted. Which format is appropriate depends on six factors that describe the expertise and facilitation skills of the trainer. See the Guide to Select Lesson Plans on the following page.

There are also 15 suggestions on page 78 in the Develop Lesson Plan Checklist that can be used to evaluate the effectiveness and completeness of a lesson plan.

# GUIDE TO SELECT TYPES OF LESSON PLANS

- SCRIPTED lesson plan:    provides a written narrative for the instructor to use, has complete lectures and answers to activities.

- OUTLINE lesson plan:    provides learning objectives, description of activities and special notes for content outside awareness of the instructor.

- OVERVIEW lesson plan:    lists learning objectives and activities with time frames and material required.

The amount of detail to include in a lesson plan depends on the six factors listed below. Given a specific subject or class, rate each point on a five-point scale or as directed for that factor:

1 = significant, 2 = above average, 3 = average, 4 = awareness, 5 = minimal or none

_____ 1. The subject matter expertise of the instructor

_____ 2. The instructor's knowledge of the adult learning process

_____ 3. The instructor's comfort with facilitating groups

_____ 4. The instructor's experience in customizing examples and/or answering questions about how to apply workshop information back on the job

_____ 5. The need to have the content of the workshop delivered *consistently* at each presentation (5 = great need or requirement, 1 = little need)

_____ 6. The choice for the participant to enroll in the workshop was made by:

    — the supervisor of the participant (5 points)

    — joint decision of supervisor and participant (3 points)

    — the participant (1 point)

_____ Total points


Recommendation for lesson plan construction:

    19–24 points = scripted lesson plan

    9–18 points = outline lesson plan

    0–8 points = overview lesson plan

# DEVELOP LESSON PLANS CHECKLIST

*Use these 15 components to evaluate your lesson plan for completeness and effectiveness:*

_____ 1. Background information on why and how this course was developed

_____ 2. Summary of the target audience for whom this course is intended

_____ 3. Type of lesson plan to be developed (scripted, outline, overview)

_____ 4. Overview of course content

_____ 5. Any special information about course strategy

_____ 6. Behavioral objectives

_____ 7. Specific limited content to complete objectives

_____ 8. Alternative activities, prioritized for individualizing instruction or dealing with time constraints

_____ 9. Selection of learning activities that are appropriate for the objective

_____ 10. Description of learning activities

_____ 11. Enough practice to develop knowledge, skills, or attitudes

_____ 12. A means to evaluate learning

_____ 13. Recommended time frames for each activity, including breaks (15-minute pacing)

_____ 14. Transitions for each activity

_____ 15. Summary of learning points

# Chapter 7

## How to Hire a Consultant or External Trainer

### Objectives

- Find the right kind of consulting help.
- Learn how to interview a consultant.
- Learn how to select the best consultant or trainer.
- Learn how to negotiate and hire.
- Learn how to monitor external consultants.

### Chapter Tools

- Screen Consultants Criteria Worksheet
- Proposal Evaluation Rating Sheet
- Consultant Interview Questions
- Consultant Interview Evaluation Checklist
- Decision Making and Negotiation Checklist
- How to Monitor Consultant Performance
- Consulting Closing Checklist

## Questions

Answer this question to identify your current development level for the issues addressed in this chapter:

1. *Which stage of development describes how external consultants are selected?*

— Stage 1: No clear selection criteria or means exist.

— Stage 2: Selection criteria are clear. Consultants usually have extensive subject matter expertise and recent parallel client experience.

— Stage 3: Written external consultant requirements consist of knowledge of subject matter, training and process skills, and practical expertise in the field.

— Stage 4: Consulting candidates demonstrate knowledge, skills and expertise in a formal assessment process.

— Stage 5: In addition to stage 4 development, external consultants' skills are related to the organization's business needs.

If you rated yourself at Stage 1 or Stage 2 for this diagnostic question, you might want to proceed through this chapter as it is written. If you rated yourself at Stage 3 or higher, you might benefit from previewing the tools provided in this chapter before working through the ideas and suggestions provided with the checklists.

## Finding the Right Kind of Consulting Help

To find the right type of consulting help from sources outside your organization, first identify what type of help you want. Are you interested in buying a product? If so, Chapter 4 has several tools and suggestions. Are you interested in retaining consulting services? If so, develop and write your objectives in selecting an external consultant before talking to consultants. This will help maintain your focus and deter you from being drawn to a product that sounds attractive but does not meet your objective.

Think about what type of help you expect from this consultant. What roles do you want the consultant to play? Several possible roles are listed below.

• Observer who provides feedback and offers suggestions

• Facilitator who is a process consultant who can lead a group

• Questioner who gathers information, analyzes it, and provides feedback

• Problem solver who offers alternatives and helps make decisions

• Trainer who imparts new knowledge and skills

• Advisor who defines issues and offers advice and suggestions

• Director who proposes guidelines, persuades or directs and implements decisions.

## Selecting the Consultant

It may be appropriate to hire a consultant who can provide a combination of the roles described above. Once you have decided what type of consulting help you want, identify resources to locate consultants who can provide the type of service you require. Professional associations with directories of members who are professional consultants, or a search of the Web can help locate possible consultants. See Appendix B for a list of training resources to help locate the right consultant.

When contacting a consultant for the first time, create a set of screening criteria so you can narrow your search and save time, and invite qualified consultants to submit a proposal. See recommended screening criteria on the following page.

# SCREEN CONSULTANTS
# CRITERIA WORKSHEET

*Use these and other criteria, specific to your project, to qualify consultants who are willing to submit a proposal to provide the services that you want.*

1. Describe the objective the consultant will achieve through this project.

2. What are the role(s) you want the consultant to assume?

3. What type of experience does the consultant have working on this or similar projects?

4. Does the consultant have experience working in your industry?

5. What is the range of hourly and daily consulting fees this consultant charges? Is this amount within your budget?

6. Is the consultant able to meet your time requirements?

## Proposal Review and Consultant Interview Process

Sort through the consulting proposals that meet your requirements using the Proposal Rating Evaluation Sheet on page 84. Review the proposal for both mechanical concerns and content concerns. Proposals are a preview of the type of work you are likely to receive from a consultant. For example, a proposal lacking appropriate attention to detail may indicate that the consultant will not provide enough detail in the final product.

Once you have reviewed the proposals, interview the top two or three consulting candidates using the questions from the Consultant Interview Questions on page 85. It is not unusual for a senior representative of the firm to arrive at the interview, even though another junior consultant will be the one to actually provide the consulting services. Be sure you have an opportunity to meet the actual consultant who will work on your project. Use the interview criteria on page 86 to make sure your interview is complete. Use the Decision Making and Negotiations Checklist on page 87 to determine which consultant offers the best value for the proposed fee and determine whether you have negotiated an appropriate agreement.

# PROPOSAL EVALUATION
# RATING SHEET

Directions: rate the following points for each proposal you receive.

5 = outstanding, exceptional, unique approach

4 = good, satisfactory

3 = adequate, nothing special

2 = missed the mark

1 = not worth considering

0 = absent

## Mechanical Concerns

_____ 1. Attention to detail

_____ 2. Covered all areas requested in statement of work

_____ 3. Added something the buyer (you) had not considered

_____ 4. Language, syntax, spelling, and other mechanics

_____ 5. Overall professional appearance

_____ 6. Ideas presented expressed clearly

## Content Concerns

_____ 7. Responsibility for tasks clearly fixed

_____ 8. Objectives of project understood and addressed appropriately

_____ 9. Appropriate methodology suggested for this project

_____ 10. Clear statement of what work included or excluded

_____ 11. Appropriate method of evaluating the project

_____ 12. Realistic time schedule proposed

_____ 13. Fees clearly itemized, fee schedule (daily, hourly) of fixed price costs

_____ 14. Specific personnel identified with appropriate experience

_____ 15. Means to check references available

    — Results achieved

    — Flexibility of consultant

    — Timeliness of previous project completion

_____ 16. Enough information to make a decision

# CONSULTANT INTERVIEW QUESTIONS

*Use the following questions as a guideline for interviewing a prospective external consultant.*

- What is your understanding of this project?

- Given our objectives, how do your services match our needs?

- What are the skills that you can apply to this project?

- What are examples of past projects on which you used these skills?

- What organizations in our industry have you worked for as a consultant?

- Where have you worked with employees similar to ours in job tasks and responsibilities?

- What additional information do you need from us to refine a proposal for this project?

- When can you begin work on this project?

- From the personnel identified in the proposal, who will act as project manager and who will actually do the consulting work on this project?

- Are you willing to customize your services for this project? At what cost?

- How will you measure the results of your work for us?

- What are the project deliverables?

- Do you have your own letter of agreement, or are you willing to accept our letter of agreement and/or purchase order as a contract?

# CONSULTANT INTERVIEW EVALUATION CHECKLIST

*Use these criteria for selecting a training consultant to provide services to your organization. What other criteria can you suggest to add to this list?*

_____ 1. What is my initial reaction to the consultant as a person? How easy or difficult will it be to work with this person? Is the consultant likeable?

_____ 2. What is the consultant's interest level in this project? How can you tell?

_____ 3. Does this person have any annoying mannerisms that may detract from the training or the project?

_____ 4. Would the target population group accept this consultant as credible?

_____ 5. After your initial explanation of your need, does the consultant ask questions or immediately begin to provide all the answers?

_____ 6. Will you have an opportunity to see this consultant in action, either live or on tape?

_____ 7. Does the consultant's objectives, content, and target audience fit the objectives, target audience, and content you have in mind?

_____ 8. Will the consultant customize the program to suit your needs? Is there a cost to customize the materials?

_____ 9. Is the consultant willing to give you a written proposal at no charge?

_____ 10. Were there any negative cues you picked up during the interview?

_____ 11. Did the consultant "push" for a close at the end of the interview?

## DECISION MAKING AND NEGOTIATION CHECKLIST

*Use this process to help decide which consultant will provide the best value for services and be sure you have negotiated the best conditions and rates.*

_____ 1. Do the consultant's proposed services meet your objectives?

_____ 2. Have you compared this consultant's fees to at least two others?

_____ 3. Has the consultant provided references for similar work and for clients in your industry?

_____ 4. Have you called the references provided by this consultant to find out the quality of the consultant's work and the nature of the working relationship the reference had with the consultant?

_____ 5. Have the fees been "unbundled" so you know individual costs and exactly what is included in all costs?

_____ 6. Are there parts of the project that you can provide internally that are a better fit for your organization? Will completing these parts of the project internally reduce the consultant's fee?

_____ 7. Is the consultant willing to make small customizations at no charge?

_____ 8. Is the consultant's fee to make major customizations reasonable?

_____ 9. Is the consultant willing to meet your time requirements?

_____ 10. Does this consultant seem flexible?

_____ 11. Does this consultant seem knowledgeable?

_____ 12. Does this consultant seem reliable and honest?

## Monitoring the Consultant's Work

Once work begins on the project, use the checklist on the following page to monitor the consultant's performance to make sure you are getting the results expected. The key to working successfully with an external consultant is to communicate openly and often. Share your understanding of the project and your expectations frequently. Clarify and verify your assumptions. Finally, when the project is coming to a close, use the Consultant Closing Checklist on page 90 to close out the project. If there were some unexpected events, what did you learn from this experience that you can use to monitor future projects better?

**HOW TO MONITOR CONSULTANT PERFORMANCE**

## Beginning

_____ 1. Discuss the written scope of work with the consultant, and clearly identify expectations, deliverables, and timeline for the project.

_____ 2. Explore assumptions and boundaries that need clarification for the project.

_____ 3. Agree on resources each party will provide.

_____ 4. Identify first steps and when additional approvals or reviews are needed.

_____ 5. Agree on the deadline and content of the first status report.

_____ 6. Complete formal contracting process required by your organization.

_____ 7. Understand how changes can be made to the project.

## Interim Monitoring and Project Management Using Status Reports

_____ 8. Identify the progress toward task completion.

_____ 9. Review accomplishments to date.

_____ 10. Review issues requiring discussion and resolution.

_____ 11. Review the budget.

_____ 12. Share concerns and expectations to be resolved before the next status report or end of the project.

_____ 13. Resolve project change issues.

## Closing the Project

_____ 14. Terminate the project with a final meeting with the consultant.

_____ 15. Document all phases of the project and deliverables with a written report from the consultant.

_____ 16. Acknowledge, publicize, and celebrate successes.

# CONSULTING CLOSING CHECKLIST

Which of these questions might be appropriate to finish working with a consultant?

_____ 1. Did the deliverables meet the objectives?

_____ 2. Did the results meet the specifications in the scope of work?

_____ 3. Is the "client" using the products or services delivered by the consultant?

_____ 4. Did the project conclude on time?

_____ 5. Did the project stay within budget?

_____ 6. Could project changes have been anticipated and/or avoided? If so, how?

_____ 7. Were issues handled appropriately by the consultant? By you?

_____ 8. Did the consultant lay the groundwork for continued success?

_____ 9. What was learned during this project that can be applied elsewhere?

_____ 10. Do the results provide the expected return on investment or bottom line results?

_____ 11. Are your internal customers satisfied with the outcomes and process such that they are willing to work with the consultant again?

_____ 12. Would you hire this consultant again? Why or why not?

## Chapter 8

# How to Begin to Market Training Internally

## Objectives

- Learn how to market training services.

- Learn the difference between selling vs. marketing.

- Learn the difference between marketing services vs. products.

- Create a partnership with supervisors to avoid "no shows" at training events.

## Chapter Tools

- Marketing Events Checklist

- Avoid "No Shows" Tips and Checklist

## Questions

Use these two questions to identify your current development level for the issues addressed in this chapter.

1. *Which stage of development describes how training is marketed in the organization?*
   — Stage 1: The training function "sells" courses to internal clients from existing products or services.
   — Stage 2: The training function investigates the need for training and selects courses designed to meet the business need.
   — Stage 3: The training function conducts a regular needs assessment to be sure training courses are meeting the current needs.
   — Stage 4: The training function systematically uses a marketing approach to provide training services.
   — Stage 5: The training function partners with operations to update existing courses and find new resources, and always promotes training that meets the business need.

2. *Which stage of development describes the extent and variety of the marketing effort?*
   — Stage 1: The training function makes no effort to promote training beyond the person or group who requests the event or course.
   — Stage 2: The training function uses a variety of methods to attract those who might benefit from scheduled training.
   — Stage 3: The training function uses various methods that demonstrate the benefits of training to the learner and how to use what is learned, while promoting the event at least three months before it occurs.
   — Stage 4: The training function systematically enlists help from supervisors to promote training, has personal ambassadors promote training with testimonials, and publishes successes of past training participants.
   — Stage 5: The training function partners with supervisors and line managers to improve awareness of training events. Unique methods promote training including learning contracts, open house events, and publishing the function's training plan.

If you rated yourself at Stage 1 or Stage 2 for most of these diagnostic questions, you might want to proceed through this chapter as it is written. If you rated yourself at Stage 3 or higher, you might benefit from previewing the tools provided in this chapter before working through the ideas and suggestions provided with the checklists.

## What Is Marketing?

Successfully marketing training to the organizations requires learning what training needs exist and finding the resources to meet them. Marketing training is a proactive approach to running the training department that gives the department a greater opportunity to meet training needs through planning, rather than allowing events to occur by conducting individual training events as requested.

Selling training successfully means that when an internal customer requests a training program, the training department encourages the customer to "buy" what is already available, whether or not it is the best solution to the need behind the training request.

## Marketing Success Factors

To be successful in marketing training to the organization, keep in mind three factors:

1. Who are your customers?

2. What are your customers' training needs, and how do they relate to business needs?

3. Are you marketing training services or products?

If you know who your customers are, you can anticipate their needs. Getting to know your customers entails attending their staff meetings in order to find out what is happening that might affect their requests for training. Identifying their needs will allow you to relate them to the organization's business needs, which in turn will bring successful results to the forefront. Finally, identify whether you are marketing training services or products. Training services need to be marketed differently from products because training services

- Are bought primarily to solve problems.

- Require the use of different marketing methods and strategies.

- Must be marketed on an ongoing basis.

## Marketing Techniques

Use the following ideas to market training services on an ongoing basis:

1. Attend managers' meetings, discuss how you may help them reach their business objectives, and keep them informed about the accomplishments of the training department.

2. Stay in touch with your organization's business. Network with managers every chance you get. Go to lunch once a month with a key person in another department, and find out what others do and how you might help them do it better.

3. Involve managers in whatever way you can. Hold training department open houses with refreshments. Invite managers to the training department and ask them to make suggestions, and give them marketing materials and resources to take away. Show a video of the training department's philosophy and how it furthers the organization's mission.

4. Create recognition programs for those managers who do all the right things when it comes to supporting the training of their people. Hold a recognition luncheon and give certificates of recognition. Send a list of names to the president for recognition and publish their names in your newsletter.

Training provides a service to the organization; individuals who provide a service need to constantly remind their customers of their services. Use the ideas on the Marketing Events Checklist on the next page to promote the services of the training department and keep the image of the customer present.

# MARKETING EVENTS CHECKLIST

*For each training event, use these techniques to promote the event and as a means to keep the training department's services visible to the internal customer.*

1. Use "brag boards" (prominently displayed representations of the accomplishments of the department). Show pictures of trainees, testimonials from reaction sheets and letters, and summaries of reaction sheets in graph form.

2. Publish the department's accomplishments in the company's newsletters, video magazines, etc. Start your own newsletter to keep people up to date on what's happening. Be sure to share the WIIFM (what's in it for me) of training.

3. Develop a "look" of your own for the training department by using a slogan and creating a mission statement or a logo, and publish them every chance you get. Use your own color of paper for workshop announcements.

4. Use pictures, pictures, and more pictures.

5. Provide additional services to the organization such as making overhead transparencies for presentation or publishing the company newsletter. Monitor training attendance and send reports to management.

## Avoid "No Shows" at Training Events

Proper planning can avoid presenting a training event that is poorly attended. Once you have created a partnership with line managers (as suggested in Chapter 2), share the responsibilities of marketing the program with the line managers and supervisors of the participants. Use the Avoid No Shows Tips and Checklist on the following pages to reduce the risk of having poor attendance at the training event.

# AVOID "NO SHOWS" TIPS AND CHECKLIST

*Use this checklist to plan a training event. Start planning at least six to eight weeks prior to the date the training will be held.*

## Six to Eight Weeks before the Program Date

_____ 1. Make arrangements:

— Select program date.

— Select program site.

— Survey site for size, ventilation and heat, furniture, lighting.

— Is transportation needed for participants?

— Is adequate parking available?

— Reserve the training room, identify room setup.

— Order audiovisual (AV) equipment (screen, projectors, etc).

— Order refreshments, lunch.

_____ 2. Develop workshop announcement copy and format (letter, brochure):

— Copy shows benefits and outcomes, not just content.

— Include an outline of the subjects covered.

— Use testimonials of others who have participated in program.

— Include a cover letter from top management to announce and *endorse* the program, including reason for training.

— Pinpoint "take home" results for the participant.

— Balance personal benefits with organizational benefits.

## Six Weeks before the Program Date

_____ 1. Send the announcement:

— Send or e-mail to individuals in target group.

— Send or e-mail to supervisor of target group.

— Post announcement on Web page or bulletin board with directions to enroll.

— Insert announcement in newsletter or company bulletin.

— Send with return enrollment card (signed by supervisor and the participant).

## Six Weeks to One Week before the Program Date

_____ 1. Keep a log of attendees and their supervisors.

_____ 2. Acknowledge the following in writing to the participant and the supervisor:

— Name of participant enrolled

— Location of classroom (include off-site map)

— Title of class

— Date of workshop and times

— Include any pre-work assignments and preparation lists

_____ 3. Keep a standby list of those who want to attend, but are not representative of the exact target population. Expect up to 20 percent cancellation on the day of the workshop. Fill in with standbys. Some organizations collect a $5 registration fee (personal check or payroll deduction form) that is returned to the participants when they arrive at the workshop.

_____ 4. Duplicate handout materials.

## One to Two Days before the Program Date

_____ 1. Telephone or e-mail the participants and remind them of the training program. Get renewed commitment that they will attend.

_____ 2. Send the supervisor a list of his or her personnel attending the program. This notice should be delivered the day before the training as a polite reminder.

_____ 3. Reconfirm all room, food, AV, and other arrangements. Most hotels require a 72-hour guarantee/confirmation for food and room setup.

_____ 4. Prepare a workshop packet for the instructor with name badges or tent cards, sign-in sheet, evaluation forms, handouts, roster of participants, copy of hotel information, etc. (See sample checklist on page 139.)

## The Day of the Program

_____ 1. Arrive early to attend to last minute arrangements.

_____ 2. Check room setup and refreshments.

_____ 3. Test all equipment, and check for spare bulbs.

_____ 4. Tape electrical cords to the floor with duct tape.

_____ 5. Put out handout materials, paper, pencils, etc.

_____ 6. Set up registration and sign-in table.

## Following the Program

_____ 1. Record attendance on employee data base/transcripts.

_____ 2. Create a trend analysis from reaction sheet information (see page 186).

_____ 3. Send or make a presentation of a summary of the reaction sheets to management.

_____ 4. Respond to any negative comments with phone calls or visits as needed.

_____ 5. Send a copy of the group photograph to all participants.

_____ 6. Make follow-up visits to participants and supervisors to learn of success stories following training. Write an article for the company newsletter about the success.

_____ 7. Make course design corrections as needed.

Chapter 9

# How to Publicize Training Events

## Objectives

- Prepare training announcements, course catalogs, and brochures.

- Create benefit statements to help "sell" training internally.

- Create newsletters, bulletin boards, and e-mail training announcements.

- Use a variety of methods to publicize training events.

- Publicize the services available from the training function.

- Use numbers and graphics to demonstrate and publicize training results and successes.

- Use recognition tools for those who support training.

- Use marketing information to develop future training plans.

- Use brown bag seminars to market training.

## Chapter Tools

- Dynamite Flyers and Brochures Checklist

- Graphic Guidelines for Brochures

- Training Announcement Template

- Publicity Checklist

- Training Department Services

- Publicize Training Results Template

- Recognition Tools

## Questions

Use these questions to identify your current development level for the issues addressed in this chapter.

1. *Which stage of development describes the use of training brochures and catalogs?*

   — Stage 1: The training department creates a brief announcement for existing training, published through e-mail, and announces training events at regular meetings.

   — Stage 2: The training department prepares individual brochures to identify when and where training will be held. Newsletters and bulletin boards also announce training events along with e-mail and the supervisor's assistance.

   — Stage 3: The training department publishes a course catalog of offerings on at least a quarterly basis. Offerings identify the target audience, benefits of training, and how to enroll. The training department maintains a Web page that promotes training.

   — Stage 4: Training brochures and catalogs include testimonials and successes of past participants. Pictures, graphics, and a training department logo create a signature look in promotional materials. Employees can register online or via fax, telephone, or mail.

   — Stage 5: The training department's branding is extensively used to promote programs. Feedback on the success of different marketing materials is tracked. Trend analysis identifies which brochures are most successful.

2. *What is the stage of development for the methods used to publicize training events?*

   — Stage 1: Little to no means are used to publicize training events. Employees are often notified on the day of training to attend a specific program.

   — Stage 2: Training events are publicized through memo and e-mail announcements to the target population.

   — Stage 3: Each training event is publicized using a variety of methods such as brochures, bulletin boards, letters of invitation, staff meeting announcements, memos, and e-mails.

   — Stage 4: A systematic approach is used in partnership with supervisors and managers to publicize events both individually and clustered.

   — Stage 5: In addition to the systematic approach used at Stage 4, creative and innovative methods are used to promote training, such as contests, incentives, and use of personal ambassadors in each department.

If you rated yourself at Stage 1 or Stage 2 for most of these diagnostic questions, you might want to proceed through this chapter as it is written. If you rated yourself at Stage 3 or higher, you might benefit from previewing the tools provided in this chapter before working through the ideas and suggestions provided with the checklists.

# Training Announcements and Brochures

Training announcements and brochures attract employees to attend workshops if they

1. Relay the right message

2. Are well-designed graphically

3. Are delivered in a timely manner

The right message is one that appeals to the reader. Studies show that the title of a workshop is very important in determining whether the potential learner is willing to read the brochure. Use key words in the workshop title like "how to" to demonstrate practicality and usefulness. Words like "you" and "your" in the title personalize the appeal of the workshop. If the potential learner's job title appears in the title it says, "this workshop is for YOU!" A workshop titled "The Professional Trainer" brought a reasonable number of participants to a workshop for new trainers. When the title was changed to "Survival Skills for the New Trainer" attendance increased dramatically.

Titles three to five words in length that are snappy and appealing tend to draw more learners into the workshop than longer titles. If more than five words are needed to describe the title appropriately, use a subtitle to clarify what is in a workshop.

Brochures need to identify the benefits of attending training to highlight value and attract potential learners. Benefit statements are presented from the learner's perspective and emphasize what the *learner* gets out of training and offer solutions to his or her problems. Training benefits are viewed individually, not universally, so the benefit must appeal to each individual reading the brochure. Here are some examples of benefit statements:

- In this session, you will identify how to use Adult Learning principles to speed the rate of learning.

- You can increase sales and customer satisfaction by matching the right product to the needs of your customer.

- You will increase your confidence in dealing with difficult people.

Another element of the "right" message means providing enough information about the content and the methods used in the training program. Be sure to list enough information in bullet point format so that it is easy to read. Also, identify the appropriate target audience for the workshop. Tell the learner whether this workshop is for beginning, intermediate, or advanced learners, or for anyone. Listing prerequisites or asking a few short questions about prior knowledge, skills, or experience as part of the brochure copy may help determine the appropriate level of instruction. Be sure to include the time and place of the workshop to help participants plan to attend the workshop for the entire course. Briefly describe the instructor for the workshop and his or her credentials and experience to teach this particular workshop. The Dynamite Flyers and Brochures Checklist on the next page lists all the elements of good brochure design.

# DYNAMITE FLYERS AND BROCHURES CHECKLIST

*Use this checklist to be sure each training flyer or brochure makes a quality statement about each training event.*

_____ 1. Does all information in the brochure send a clear and consistent message?

_____ 2. Does the title consist of five words or less and use a subtitle for further information? Does the title contain practical "how to" words? Does the title contain a job title or the words "you" or "your" to personalize the workshop?

_____ 3. Does your training department use its own logo to create a consistent image?

_____ 4. Is class content, objective, and benefits information prominently displayed?

_____ 5. Does the brochure include registration information?

_____ 6. Do you create a sense of "newness" to your programs without compromising consistency?

_____ 7. Do you use testimonials to promote new training events?

_____ 8. Are pictures and graphics appropriate for your message?

_____ 9. Are fonts, layout, and colors appropriate?

_____ 10. Can you offer a "bonus" for those who sign up early?

_____ 11. Is just enough information provided in an attractive format or is the reader bogged down by too much information?

_____ 12. Do you ask someone else to proofread your work?

_____ 13. Do you send out follow-up mailings?

_____ 14. Do you use a variety of distribution methods?

_____ 15. Can your training program compete with outside vendors for quality, timing, and meeting employee needs?

Create a well-designed graphically appealing brochure. See the color checklist on the next page to identify the graphic appeal of different colors used in brochures. When selecting colors for a brochure, remember that colored paper, not just ink, also makes a difference. Single-color brochures are often the least expensive to create. Create graphic interest in single-color brochures by using screens. When creating two-color brochures, be sure to select colors that harmonize. Use a dark black, brown, purple, or blue as the primary color and select a strong and brilliant color as an accent color. Again, use screens and reverse type to create graphic interest and accents. If your budget allows for more expensive four-color brochures, use the amount of restraint and understatement appropriate for your organization. Let the message come across in the descriptions of the training event instead of being overpowered by colors and graphics.

To maintain graphic appeal and promote readability, it is best to use no more than two different fonts, plus bold and italic versions of the same fonts, and no more than two to three different sizes of these fonts. Select one size for headlines and another size for basic copy. Details can be provided in small type, but note that type sizes of less than nine points are difficult for most people to read.

The most commonly used font is Times Roman. This font has serifs or "feet" at the bottom of the letters. A sans serif font (e.g., Arial or Tahoma) can be attractive when used in headlines. Use **bold face** fonts for emphasis and use *italics* for quotations. Emphasis can be added by creating headlines in all capital letters.

# GRAPHIC GUIDELINES FOR BROCHURES

*Use these guidelines to make brochures and flyers graphically appealing.*

Colors for brochures:

| Color | Meaning or Reaction to This Color | Suggested Use in Brochures |
|-------|-----------------------------------|----------------------------|
| Green | Analytical, precise, brings out opinions, resistance to change | Accent color |
| Blue | Calm sensation, traditional, reduces blood pressure, easiest to read | Accent color for headlines, background for screens |
| Red | Power, impact, increase pulse, intensity, impulsive, desire, passion | Accents only |
| Yellow | Bright, cheerful, hope, restless, anxiety if used too much, seeks change | Accent or to lighten darker colors |
| Purple | Mystical, magic, delight, light-hearted, unrealistic, immature | Accent color, can be good as a second color or for screens |
| Black | Dark, threatening, somber, can have negative meaning if overused. | Makes copy easy to read, harder to read in "reverse" Use as an accent |
| White | Clear, pure, absence of color | Use as a background color and to add space to make copy stand out. |

Fonts

\_\_\_ Use no more than two different fonts

\_\_\_ Use capital letters for headlines and emphasis

\_\_\_ Use different fonts consistently for the same type of copy

\_\_\_ Use black, brown, purple or dark blue for font color

\_\_\_ Do not use fonts smaller than nine-point type

Another way to make brochures and flyers attractive is to deliver them in a timely manner. Most people lead busy lives and need to plan to attend training one to two months ahead of the event. If employees receive a brochure six to eight weeks prior to the event, attendance will be larger than if you wait until one month prior to the event to send them out. Of course, there are exceptions to this suggestion, especially if employees have little discretionary time.

Mailing brochures to the target population as well as the supervisors of the intended audience can help promote better attendance at training events. Send preview announcements to "save the date" of the event before preparing and distributing the brochure, and send follow-up announcements or repeated mailings to sway those who could not make up their minds when they received the first copy of the brochure.

The three elements of well-written brochures apply to announcements that appear in newsletters, on bulletin boards, or in e-mails. See further suggestions for techniques to publicize training events, following the template on the following page, to include all the elements of a well-written brochure.

# TRAINING ANNOUNCEMENT TEMPLATE

| WORKSHOP TITLE HERE WITH "HOW TO" FOR YOUR AUDIENCE | GRAPHIC OR PICTURE HERE |
|---|---|

**WHO SHOULD ATTEND**
(list by job title or describe duties)

**WORKSHOP CONTENT**

Unit 1:
- 
- 
- 

Unit 2:
- 
- 
- 

Unit 3:
- 
- 
- 

Unit 4:
- 
- 
- 

**WHAT YOU'LL LEARN**

List benefit statements that describe what the learner gets from this workshop:

✓
✓
✓
✓
✓
✓
✓
✓

**WORKSHOP LEADER**

Describe the credentials and expertise of the workshop leader.

**REGISTRATION INFORMATION**

Date, time, and place of workshop

Register for the workshop by:
Telephone
Fax
E-mail
For questions, contact:

**TESTIMONIALS FROM PAST PARTICIPANTS**

(Describe personal reaction to the workshop material, skills of the facilitator, how new skills were used, how much this type of training is needed in our organization.)

## Training Announcements

It takes a number of repeated announcements to attract a single customer. Therefore, training departments need to identify methods to reach potential learners. Take advantage of existing lines of communication. If your organization has an "official announcement" mechanism (such as bulletins, newsletters, memos, announcements of regularly scheduled meetings, and meeting minutes), use it to notify potential learners of a training event and where to find more details about the event.

Publish announcements on physical and electronic bulletin boards. Place brief announcements in paycheck envelopes. Maintain a training department Web site and send broadcast e-mail announcements which may attract a secondary audience that might not get the "official" announcement, invitation, or brochure. One high-tech organization sent a broadcast e-mail to the immediate company and its off-site facilities and was surprised to find interest from their overseas branches. The overseas employees were able to benefit from the program and even took materials back to their site and trained their co-workers.

# PUBLICITY CHECKLIST

1. Select one or more of the following means to distribute training announcements:

   — Organization's official announcement mechanism

   — Company bulletins

   — Company bulletin boards

   — Electronic bulletin boards

   — Company and/or department newsletters

   — Meeting announcement mechanisms

   — Meeting minutes

   — Paycheck envelopes

   — Personal invitation or letter

2. Identify the lead time each delivery mechanism requires so the announcement reaches the target audience six to eight weeks prior to the event.

3. Get a tentative count from each delivery mechanism "custodian" to identify how many announcements to print. Gain agreement from others responsible to make distributions on your behalf.

4. Identify managers and supervisors who are willing to support the training event and provide testimonials or act as sponsors of the training event.

5. Test market the announcement by asking individuals from the target audience to review and critique the training event announcement.

6. Prepare the announcement using the template provided in this chapter.

7. Prepare a cover letter or introduction from the sponsor of the event.

8. Distribute the brochure and cover letter or announcement to the primary and secondary audiences who will benefit from the training.

## Publicize a Variety of Services

Because the training department focuses primarily on offering services such as training workshops and presentations, the other services available from the training function might need ongoing publicity to promote their use. Offering a variety of services can create positive interest in the training function and promote attendance at training events. Use the checklist on the following page for suggestions about services that your training department might provide.

## Publicize Training Results

The training department will receive support as long as others agree that training gets results. Chapter 15 shows techniques to measure the results of training. Suggestions that follow here identify how to publicize those results to build the training function's reputation and attendance at future training events. Use the template on page 111 for information on how to capture and publicize some of the training results.

## Use Recognition Tools

When publicizing training results, include awards and recognition for those who support training functions and events. Those who are recognized by the training function and by their peers are more likely to continue supporting training events. See the variety of recognition tools on page 112.

## Brown Bag Seminars

Brown bag seminars are brief training events that happen over a meal. You can use these events to showcase or preview upcoming training events. Give a 10-minute preview, distribute a one-page handout, and discuss one idea from the training program. This will pique the interest of potential participants and increase enrollment at training events.

# TRAINING DEPARTMENT SERVICES

Training and development personnel in your organization could provide the following services:

- Creating overhead transparencies or electronic visuals and graphics for company presentations

- Collecting feedback from employees who attend outside training events conducted by commercial providers and can recommend attendance at worthwhile events

- Researching appropriate audiovisual equipment requirements and suppliers for internal use

- Identifying appropriate off-site meeting and training facilities

- Coordinating off-site meetings and events

- Providing a reprint order service to management

- Providing a clipping service for topics of interest to management

- Providing benchmarking information about competitors and allied industries

- Providing meeting facilitators

- Writing articles for company newsletters and/or industry journals

- Writing or developing presentations for executives and managers for use at internal or external meetings

- Making travel arrangements for employees who go to off-site meetings

- Making hotel reservations for those who travel to your location for training events

- Providing access to company e-mail and voice mail to employees who attend training events at your location

- Providing a map and list of area restaurants for out-of-town trainees

# PUBLICIZE TRAINING RESULTS TEMPLATE

Following training, quantify the types of information below, convert these numbers to graphic pictures, and then publicize the results.

- Saves Time
- Saves Money
- Improves Work Flow
- Decreases Waiting Time
- Improves Product Quality
- Improves Communication
- Supports Mission and Core Values
- Improves Appearance
- Saves Supplies
- Decreases Customer Complaint
- Improves Safety
- Improves Job Satisfaction
- Provides Faster Service
- Eliminates a Repetitious Process

**Publicize results by**

- Announcing results at management meetings
- Writing an article for the company newsletter
- Writing a letter to the sponsor and manager of those attending training
- Posting results on bulletin boards, including electronic bulletin boards and intranets
- Awarding prizes and certificates to best in appropriate categories of results
- Offering discounts to attend future training events

# RECOGNITION TOOLS

Use these recognition tools to reward and encourage those who support the training function.

- Hold a recognition luncheon.

- Give certificates of recognition.

- Send a list of names to the company's president for recognition.

- Publish their names in your newsletter.

- Create awards in appropriate categories.

- Use company merchandise as awards.

- Award certificates of completion.

- Create a certificate program and acknowledge those who reach significant milestones in their development.

- Take photographs of those who gain results and support training. Circulate pictures to the participants, hang them in the company hallways, and publish them in the company newsletter and on the company intranet.

Chapter 10

# How to Set Up and Maintain Your Company's Training Web Site

## Objectives

- Determine what type of training information should be on your Web page.

- Find appropriate training links.

- Determine how often to maintain the Web site.

- Review cautions for Web-based training.

## Chapter Tools

- Training Web Page Content Checklist

- Types of Training Web Links

## Question

Use this question to identify your current development level for the issues addressed in this chapter.

1. *What stage of development describes the type of training information on your Web page?*

    — Stage 1: The training department does not have a Web page.

    — Stage 2: The training department posts information on the organization's intranet, but does not have its own Web page.

    — Stage 3: The training department has its own Web page that describes the content and objectives of its workshops and other services.

    — Stage 4: The training department's Web page is systematically maintained and updated on a regular basis.

    — Stage 5: The training department's Web page is continually improved with links to other sites, new features, activities, resources, and benefits.

If you rated yourself at Stage 1 or Stage 2 for most of these diagnostic questions, you might want to proceed through this chapter as it is written. If you rated yourself at Stage 3 or higher, you might benefit from previewing the tools provided in this chapter before working through the ideas and suggestions provided with the checklists.

## Characteristics of Training Department Web Pages

Training department Web pages are helpful and useful if they provide complete and timely information. See the checklist on the following page for the suggested types of information and the options that you can include on your Web page. See the previous chapter (page 110) for a list of possible Training Function Services to offer, and identify how many of them can be described on your Web page and/or accessed through your Web page.

A review of the Training Department Services can also help you decide which links are appropriate to show on your Web page. See the suggestions in Appendix B for possible links to include on your Web page.

Your internal Web page can be a helpful place for an employee to begin researching a specific issue or problem. Update the training department Web page at least twice a month and show the date of the latest update. The more information available on your Web page, the more frequently it should be updated. The more often the page is updated, the more employees will access the page to find out what new services are available.

**TRAINING WEB PAGE
CONTENT CHECKLIST**

## Suggested Types of Information

Main headings or "buttons" are as follows:

- Workshop content outlines and learning objectives
- Current schedule with dates and locations for workshops
  - Maps
  - Driving directions
  - Check-in and security procedures
- Biographic information about instructors
- Certification programs
- How to register for a workshop
- How to arrange for a custom workshop for a specific group
- Custom services
  - Training needs assessments
  - Assistance in developing training plans and proposals
  - Create graphics and visuals for a presentation
  - Check out equipment
  - Assistance in purchasing training-related equipment
  - Create a custom course to meet a specific need
  - Arrange off-site meetings

**Other types of services include**

- Resource articles
- Downloadable company forms and templates with completion directions
- Links to related sites
- Tuition reimbursement program information
- Recommended books and bibliographies from past courses
- Tests and quizzes to assess skills to meet prerequisites for specific courses
- Listing of training videotapes available
- Summary of evaluations by those who have attended external training courses

- Ability to look up your own transcript of past courses attended
- Testimonials from past participants for your workshops
- Training policies
- How to send an e-mail to the training department
- How to request automatic notification when new information is posted on the Web page
- Counter to indicate how many visitors have seen your Web page
- Meal services available to trainees at various training facilities
- List of restaurants with menu descriptions and pricing information for workshop participants
- List of hotels that accept the company's corporate rate, with links to each hotel for reservation information

# TYPES OF TRAINING
# WEB LINKS

Different types of links can be useful for employees to reach various services. Consider placing these types of links on your training department's Web page.

- Other departments in the company

- Employee Handbook

- Downloadable forms and templates

- Professional associations for trainers

- Professional associations for the training industry

- Publishers of training-related books and articles

- Publishers of industry-related books and articles

- Search engines

- E-groups that discuss work-related topics of interest

- External vendors that provide company approved courses

- Approved on-line learning providers

## Web-Based Training

The Web training industry began around 1996. Many of the first course offerings were converted from computer-based training programs and offered over the Internet. The early years of Web-based training were mired in equipment and technology problems that discouraged participation. The expense of newer and faster equipment also deterred large numbers of users from using this medium for training.

Estimates of 50 percent of all training being computer-based by the year 2000 were never realized. If your organization is considering training over the Internet, first, research the equipment requirements and costs and compare those costs to current delivery methods.

Second, look at the results you want training to achieve. Identify whether a self-paced method (like Internet training) is the best method for your employees to gain the knowledge, skills, and attitudes intended to be the results of a training program. Often a combination of pre-course assignments completed over the Internet can make class meetings more productive.

Third, research providers of Internet training and compare the cost of various vendors. Look at the sophistication of the technology used in the self-paced lessons. Are learners being challenged to learn through a variety of activities or are learners merely reading information by turning very expensive electronic pages.

Additional information about Web-based training links can be found in Appendix B at the back of this book.

## Objectives

- Plan training events.

- Schedule training to get maximum attendance.

- Run trainee registration and confirmation systems.

- Prepare training rooms for instruction.

- Complete workshop follow-up in a timely manner.

## Chapter Tools

- Planning Checklist

- Scheduling Checklist

- Workshop Registration Form

- Training Participant Letter and Survey

- Pre-Workshop Survey

- Sample Confirmation Letter

- How to Get the Most Out of Our Workshop

- Great Expectations

- Registration Packet Checklist

- Room Set-up Diagrams: Six Suggested Seating Arrangements

- Room Preparation Checklist

- Audiovisual Hints

- Survival Kit for Training Rooms

- Instructor Feedback Sheet

- Workshop Follow-up Checklist

Chapter 11

# How to Smoothly Administer Training Events

## Questions

Use these questions to identify your current development level for the issues addressed in this chapter.

1. *Which stage of development describes how your training department selects courses and plans for specific training events?*

   — Stage 1: Administrative procedures are developed for each project on a one-time basis.

   — Stage 2: A list of courses describes training offerings. Listings are posted on bulletin boards and/or the organization's intranet.

   — Stage 3: A catalog details course offerings. Productivity statistics are used in a limited manner to identify the need for training. Training paths are established for only a few select technical target populations.

   — Stage 4: Productivity statistics are used to identify training needs. Training paths are established for all target populations.

   — Stage 5: Procedures are in place to ensure the integrity of the scheduling process, respond to user requests, and deal with complaints and unforeseen needs. Business cycles dictate the training schedule for off-peak times.

2. *How are courses scheduled?*

   — Stage 1: Courses are scheduled based on requests from the field or dictate of upper management.

   — Stage 2: Courses are scheduled based on the target population's anticipated needs.

   — Stage 3: Training is scheduled from a systematic assessment of the target population's needs.

   — Stage 4: Course schedules are based on information collected from the client's current and anticipated needs.

   — Stage 5: Procedures are in place to ensure the integrity of the scheduling process, respond to user requests, and deal with complaints and unforeseen needs. Business cycles dictate the training schedule for off-peak times.

3. *Describe the extent to which statistics are used in the scheduling process.*

   — Stage 1: No statistics are used to schedule training.

   — Stage 2: New course offerings are scheduled based on management dictate or industry requirements.

   — Stage 3: Data is collected and analyzed from training needs listed on the employees' performance appraisals and other needs analysis.

   — Stage 4: Statistical analysis of instructor productivity assures equitable work assignments and scheduling of a trainer's classroom sessions, preparation, course development, and travel time.

— Stage 5: Procedures are in place to ensure the integrity of the scheduling process, respond to user requests, and deal with complaints and unforeseen needs. Business cycles dictate the training schedule for off-peak times.

4. *Describe the registration, record-keeping, and confirmation systems for your training department.*

   — Stage 1: Minimal clerical support is focused on enrollment, registration, record-keeping, and travel requirements of trainers and participants.

   — Stage 2: Minimal attendance and minimal reporting are done when requested.

   — Stage 3: A statistical specialist keeps training data that is available and regularly reports activities to management.

   — Stage 4: Statistical data is formatted, interpreted, and distributed within the department for productivity analysis.

   — Stage 5: Statistical data is formatted, interpreted, and distributed to training users to demonstrate how the business needs are met. Administrative support explores alternative methods to report training data.

5. *How are classrooms prepared and materials support accomplished?*

   — Stage 1: Instructors prepare classrooms and provide materials for their courses.

   — Stage 2: Administrative support prepares classrooms and keeps an inventory of course materials.

   — Stage 3: Administrative support provides participant materials and word processing and duplication of the leader's guide.

   — Stage 4: Administrative support regularly anticipates and provides for the needs of internal and external trainers and participants.

   — Stage 5: Administrative support exceeds the expectations of internal and external trainers and participants. Quality and format of training materials are continually updated to be on a par with what is available commercially.

6. *What additional support services are available to your training function?*

   — Stage 1: No additional support services are provided.

   — Stage 2: Specific guidelines from trainer and participants are drafted, and commitments to projects are met on a limited basis.

   — Stage 3: A specialist is available to develop color transparencies, custom graphics, PowerPoint presentations, etc.

   — Stage 4: Specialized requests based on individual trainer needs or management instructions are met.

   — Stage 5: Specialized services are tailored to meet the needs of target groups and internal customers.

If you rated yourself at Stage 1 or Stage 2 for most of these diagnostic questions, you might want to proceed through this chapter as it is written. If you rated yourself at Stage 3 or higher, you might benefit from previewing the tools provided in this chapter before working through the ideas and suggestions provided with the checklists.

## Planning Training Events

Chapter 3 of this book describes how to develop a training plan. The type of planning discussed in this chapter is the immediate planning that takes place before each training event. The checklists and suggestions in this chapter will help the trainer set up systems and procedures to more easily handle administrative details for training events. This chapter discusses how to plan for internal training events. Chapter 12 offers checklists and suggestions for off-site training events. The suggestions from the Avoid No Shows Tips and Checklist from Chapter 8 can also help plan internal training events.

The planning checklist on the following page recommends that you complete a variety of tasks to have a successful meeting. Planning suggestions should be implemented well before the day of the training event, and another checklist suggests tasks for the day of the training event.

# PLANNING CHECKLIST

_____ 1. Review the training plan to

— Clarify business need for training

— Identify issues to address through training

— Partner with managers and supervisors of those who will attend training

— Clarify performance standards for tasks affected by this training

— Identify who will attend training and make target population decisions from page 46

— Establish learning objectives for training and agree with supervisors on the content outline

— Estimate the cost of training and gain agreement on fixed costs

— Select the training course from internal or external resources

— Schedule the training

— Identify how results will be evaluated

_____ 2. Select the instructor who will deliver the training

_____ 3. Select the classroom or training site

_____ 4. Confirm the availability of the classroom, instructor, and participants

_____ 5. Specify classroom setup and class size

_____ 6. Make travel and overnight arrangements for instructor and participants, if any

_____ 7. Order audiovisual equipment

_____ 8. Order refreshments

_____ 9. Develop a marketing plan for the event (see Chapter 9)

_____ 10. Create announcement or brochure for training event (see Chapter 9)

_____ 11. Distribute announcement of training event

_____ 12. Record enrollments as registrations for the workshop are taken

_____ 13. Confirm each registration at least two weeks prior to the training event

_____ 14. If the workshop fills rapidly, consider holding another session of this workshop and begin a new checklist

_____ 15. Duplicate materials and ship to classroom

_____ 16. Arrange for class photograph

_____ 17. Confirm room setup and refreshments

_____ 18. Prepare and send the instructor a registration information packet (see checklist on page 139)

## The Day before or Morning of Workshop

_____ 1. Set up room (unless done by others) and place materials at each participant's place (see pages 140–141).

_____ 2. Test equipment and have spare bulbs and batteries available.

_____ 3. Tape cords to the floor.

_____ 4. Give instructor or coordinator a packet of registration information and participant pre-workshop surveys.

_____ 5. Have sign-in forms ready for participants to sign.

_____ 6. Verify that catering order has been filled and refreshments are available.

_____ 7. Confirm luncheon arrangements if group will eat lunch together.

_____ 8. Leave a contact phone number for the instructor who might need to reach you during the day.

## Scheduling Training Events

The schedule of training events that meets the needs of the employees and the organization will draw the most number of participants. As you consider when to schedule training events, first identify whether the reason for conducting a training event is the result of a law passed by federal, state, or local authorities. For example, federal and state agencies require that certain industries and job sites conduct safety training on a regular basis. Establishing a routine day of the month for these meetings can preserve attendance and compliance with such laws.

Next, consider whether the scheduling of a training event is the result of company mandate. Some organizations require 40 hours of continuing education for all employees. If employees ignore this mandate until the end of the year, the schedule is likely to be heavier in the fourth quarter as the time for compliance with the training mandate draws near.

After required training has been scheduled, next consider the training needs that can be identified from requests for training listed on the annual performance appraisal forms. Schedule these requests for training when the participants are most available. Also consider the needs of professionals who want to advance their careers by taking specific required training. Most engineers have continuing education requirements to ensure that they remain current in their profession. Medical professionals are also required to complete a specific number of hours per year to keep their licenses current.

When scheduling is the result of a formal needs assessment that is driven by a business need, it is easy to schedule classes that employees want to attend. The checklist on the following page offers additional considerations for deciding when to schedule training events.

# SCHEDULING CHECKLIST

Identify the priority for the source of the need for this training event.

_____ Federal, state, or local laws require this training.

_____ Company mandate requires this training.

_____ This topic is frequently requested on performance appraisal forms.

_____ This topic is a required part of career ladder advancement.

_____ This topic comes from a formal needs assessment.

Scheduling considerations include

_____ What are the time requirements for the completion of training?

_____ How many participants are in the target population group?

_____ What is the recommended class size to meet the learning objectives for this group?

_____ How many sessions need to be scheduled for this group?

_____ What hours are typical for training?

_____ Is more than one work shift involved in training?

_____ See other target population decisions on page 48.

_____ If this course is one in a sequence, do participants need to attend training in a specific order?

_____ Blank out holidays and heavy vacation weeks.

_____ Blank out other days or weeks when the demands of the business will not allow employees to be away from work.

_____ Which classroom facilities will be used for this training?

_____ How many internal instructors are needed to conduct this training event?

_____ Which trainers are most skilled at presenting this type of training?

_____ Can entire work groups be released for training at the same time, or do different work groups need to attend a single session of this training?

_____ What statistical information is available from formal/informal needs assessments and/or from performance appraisal information?

_____ What are the financial implications of class size and the timing of this event?

_____ Who (by job title) needs to approve the schedule for training?

_____ What existing software tools are available to schedule training events?

_____ Is participant travel a consideration for this event? Many organizations do not ask their employees to travel on weekends to attend training events.

## Workshop Registration Process

As employees sign up for a workshop, the training department needs a registration system to keep track of the registrations, keep an accurate count for those enrolled in a specific program, and use the information for various purposes. The type of information often needed for a workshop registration is illustrated on the next page in the Workshop Registration Form.

Many commercial software programs can record the information shown in the sample form. A list of software providers is included along with sample features and outputs common to most of the software packages for sale by these providers.

When buying this type of software, ask the vendor to confirm the features and outputs you want. Most of the software vendors have demonstration disks or a Web site that demonstrates the software. Most give discounts for multiple purchases, and almost all have networked versions that allow participants to register themselves online.

# WORKSHOP REGISTRATION FORM

Name _____ Today's date _____

Company address and mail stop _____

City, State, Zip _____

Telephone _____ Fax _____

E-mail address _____

Department budget code to charge registration fee _____

Title of workshop_____

Date of workshop_____ Location _____

Objectives for attending this training:




Employee's signature _____ date _____

Supervisor's signature _____ date _____

# SOFTWARE AND RESOURCES

Software programs to schedule training and keep track of employee training records have become quite sophisticated in the past 15 years. Below are the names of eight popular programs, who sells them, and their common features. On the following pages, some of the distinguishing features are listed in a matrix for your comparison.

**The Registrar 7.06** by Pathlore
20230 Stevens Creek Blvd., Suite D
Cupertino, CA 95014-2210
*www.pathlore.com*

800-932-6311
408-446-5705 fax
*tverayo@pathlore.com*

**Ingenium 3.0** by Asymetrix Learning Systems, Inc.
95 Allens Creek Road, Bldg. 2, Suite 302
Rochester, NY 12618

800-388-7332
716-461-1989 fax

**AbraTrain — Windows 95** by HR Products Group
688 Executive Center Drive West, Suite 300
St. Petersburg, FL 33702

727-579-1111
800-487-9467 fax

**Training Wizard** by GYRUS
Experient Technical
10 S. 6th Street
Richmond, VA 23219

804-320-1414
804-359-7644 fax

**Training Partner** 2000 by GeoMetrix Data Systems, Inc.
1815 Blanshard Street, 5th Floor
Victoria, BC V8T 5A4, Canada

250-361-9300
250-361-9362 fax

**On Track for Training 5.1** by DK Systems
444 N. Michigan Avenue, Suite 3300
Chicago, IL 60611
*www.dksystems.com*

800-892-5332
312-644-2703
*sales@dksystems.com*

**TrainingOffice** by Novasys. Inc.
Tour de la Bourse
800 Place-Victoria, Ste. 2624
PO Box 151
Montreal, Quebec, Canada H4Z 1C3
*www.trainingoffice.com*

514-875-7720
514-874-9830 fax
*trainingoffice@novasys-corp.com*

**Pinnacle Learning Manager** by Learnframe
12637 South 265 West, PO Box 1409
Draper, UT 84020-1409
*www.learnframe.com*

800-738-9800
801-523-8012 fax
*mfano@learnframe.com*

## Common Features of Software

All of the software programs on the previous page have these features and outputs. Be sure to ask the producer for a demo disk, and ask about the features and outputs that are important to you. When you shop for software, be sure it is easy to learn and use, that it is flexible enough to grow with changes in your business, and that it is powerful enough to perform the functions you require.

**Features** include

- They
    — Schedule instructors

    — Schedule classes

    — Schedule classrooms/locations

    — Keep waiting lists

- Register trainees through self-registration

- Maintain employee training history

    — Skills analysis/career planning

    — Prerequisite checking

- Security

- On-line course catalogs

- On-line help

- Can operate on networks and exchange data with mainframe or other software

- Conflict checking

- Screen painting graphics

**Outputs** include

- Class rosters

- Instructor schedules

- Class schedules

- Confirmation letters

(Some products with the ability to generate custom reports and can also create sign-in sheets, certificates, and nametags. Ask each producer for details.)

All software programs operate in a Windows environment, have customer support and a hotline, provide on-site user training, and offer upgrades.

## Workshop Confirmation Process

Many on-line registration systems have an automatic confirmation feature. It may also be appropriate to ask the participant about his or her learning objectives and reason for attending the training. This type of information can be sent to the instructor prior to the class. A sample letter and survey are on pages 132–133.

At least two weeks prior to the workshop event, remind all registered participants of their commitment to attend a workshop, and provide the address and directions to the location. A sample confirmation letter appears on page 134. Depending on how difficult it may be to reach the training facility, consider enclosing a map and written directions to the workshop. It is often helpful to send such a reminder to the employee's supervisor who can support this workshop participant.

Consider sending a list of suggestions and expectations for the workshop. A sample description can be found on page 135. If participants from the same department are attending training together, consider sending a set of suggestions to the manager or supervisor to build a partnership between the manager or supervisor and the instructor of the workshop. The suggestions help prepare the participants for training and also recommend how the manager or supervisor can follow up after the training event. See pages 136–137 for how to set "Great Expectations."

When confirming workshop attendance for participants, also confirm classroom and catering arrangements, and verify that the instructor has materials and a packet of information to administer the details of the workshop. See pages 139–144 for suggestions for the contents of workshop packets.

# TRAINING PARTICIPANT LETTER
# AND SURVEY

*(To acknowledge a reservation)*

[Today's date]

[Participant's name and address]

Dear Training Professional,

Thank you for your recent registration to attend one of our [workshop name] workshops.

To help you get the most out of our workshop, please complete the attached survey and return it to us by fax as soon as possible. We will forward this information to the instructor who will be teaching your workshop.

[Insert cancellation and substitute policy]

Two weeks prior to the workshop, we will send you a confirmation letter with directions to the workshop location. If you have questions about the workshop or the survey, please give us a call [at telephone number].

Sincerely,


[Registrar's name]
Registrar

Encl. Survey

# PRE-WORKSHOP SURVEY

Please complete this survey and fax it to the training department at _____. Your answers will help us meet your objectives in attending the workshop. Thanks for taking the time to complete this survey.

Name _____     Job Title _____

Department _____     Workshop Date _____

Workshop Title _____     Workshop Location _____

Who suggested you attend this workshop?
__ My idea          __ A colleague          __ My supervisor/manager

What is your interest in this workshop? (Check all that apply.)
__ Professional development for a specific job responsibility
__ I have no previous formal training in this topic
__ This is a new job assignment
__ I am pursuing a certificate program
__ Other, specify: _____

What convinced you to attend this workshop? (Check all that apply.)
__ I've attended other company workshops
__ Content and objectives match a current need
__ Convenience of date and/or location for my current need
__ Certificate program offered from the vendor
__ Bonuses offered for this and other workshops
__ The reputation or positive report from references for this program/vendor

How long have you been involved in your current position?
__ Less than one year,__ 1–3 years, __ 4–5 years, __ 6–10 years, __ 10+ years

What are your objectives in attending this workshop?
•
•

To what extent have you discussed your objectives with your supervisor/manager?
__ Objectives have been shared and agreed upon
__ Supervisor/manager is aware of my attendance; no discussion of objectives
__ No awareness/discussion of objectives with supervisor/manager

How will you use what you learn in this workshop?
•
•

What prior classes have you attended on this subject and what organization presented those workshops?

| Year | Title of Workshop | Number of Days | Presenting Organization |
|------|-------------------|----------------|-------------------------|
|      |                   |                |                         |
|      |                   |                |                         |

# SAMPLE CONFIRMATION LETTER

*(Send two weeks before the training event.)*

[Today's date]


[Participant's Name]
[Participant's Title]
[Participant's Address]

Dear [Participant's Name],

I am pleased to confirm your reservation for our upcoming workshop:

[Workshop Title]
[Workshop City]
[Workshop Date]

The workshop will be held at the:

[Name of hotel or building]
[Address and classroom number]
[City]
[Classroom/hotel phone number]

Registration will be from [hour] to [hour], at which time the workshop will begin. The break for lunch will be at [hour]. Although lunch is not included in the program, there are restaurants in the area surrounding the hotel. The workshop ends at [hour]. Dress for this workshop is casual business attire. We recommend you bring a sweater or jacket to be comfortable in the air-conditioned meeting room.

If you know of co-workers who would benefit from this program, ask them to call to register. Although space is still available, they must act quickly.

I am certain you will have an interesting, informative learning experience. If there is anything I can do, or further questions I can answer, please contact me at [telephone number].

Sincerely,



[Name of Registrar]

encl: map

# HOW TO GET THE MOST OUT
# OF OUR WORKSHOP

*(Send these suggestions to participants with a confirmation letter.)*

1. **PLAN AHEAD**

   Tell others back at the office where you are going and that they should call the hotel's catering department if they need to get a message to you. Review the map sent with your confirmation letter and plan your route to the hotel. Some of the hotels are located near mass transit stops for your convenience. If you need further directions, please call the hotel or our office. We'll be glad to help.

2. **COME PREPARED**

   We provide an extensive handout booklet, but you may want to bring additional paper and a pen or pencil. Room temperatures fluctuate and are sometimes difficult to control. Even if the weather is warm, you may be more comfortable with a sweater or jacket. Sometimes hotels charge a parking fee and accept only cash. Lunch is not provided. We can usually suggest nearby restaurants and coffee shops.

3. **IDENTIFY YOUR GOALS**

   Think about what you want to learn from this workshop. As part of an opening activity, the instructor will help you clarify your personal objectives for attending the workshop. Are you coming to refine your skills, learn new techniques, network with your peers, etc.? If someone else enrolled you for the workshop, try to discuss his or her objectives too.

4. **BE ON TIME**

   When you arrive, check the meeting room bulletin board or ask the hotel staff for the location of our workshop. A continental breakfast is available at sign-in time from 8:30 am to 9:00 am. The workshop begins promptly at 9:00 am. The opening activity involves setting personal objectives and provides an opportunity to meet other participants. If you arrive early, there is always an opportunity to relax and chat with the instructor and others. Many instructors have a book display for your review of the latest and best training and development books.

5. **GET INVOLVED**

   [Organization name]'s workshops are noted for their involvement and for helping participants reach their personal objectives. Your questions are important to us. You can expect a day of learning-by-doing!

6. **COMPLETE AN EVALUATION FORM**

   We rely on our participants to help us improve the quality of our programs. Your comments will help us ascertain whether we have met your objectives. We welcome your suggestions.

**GREAT EXPECTATIONS**

Use the following suggestions to assist internal clients in getting the most from on-site workshops and make the event a successful, productive learning experience. Provide this summary of expectations and suggestions to management along with a written confirmation letter that describes logistics and event details. The specific workshop referenced in this form is "Meeting Planning."

## Before the Training

1. Review the outline and objectives that have been written to reflect your issues. Are there changes that should be made?

2. Meet with the participants and discuss what you see as the business need and the trends in the organization that are being met by their attendance at this course.

   — Write an invitation or announcement to the participants you expect to attend this workshop.

   — Write benefit statements (in addition to the objectives) describing how your organization and individual participants will benefit from the skills learned in the workshop.

   — Provide participants a copy of the outline with the objectives.

   This workshop should not come as a surprise. Issues about reluctant participation should surface well before the training takes place.

3. Tell participants what you expect following their attendance at this course.

   — How will they be held accountable for using these new skills?

   — What materials will they facilitate?

   — When will they facilitate?

   — Will using these new skills be observed or reviewed on a performance appraisal?

   — How will they be acknowledged and credited for their contribution?

4. Class hours are usually from 8:30 a.m. to 4:30 p.m. Do these hours need to be adjusted to meet your work hours? Earlier starting and finishing times are possible. We will need an overhead projector, flip chart with paper, and a screen. A "U" shape setting is best for a group of less than 20.

## During the Training

5. Participants should be prepared to participate and attend the workshop for the entire day. Phone calls and messages need to be handled only at breaks (one in the morning, lunchtime, and one in the afternoon). To the extent possible, compensate for workload while the employee is at training.

6. As the manager or supervisor, we need your participation at the workshop for the entire day. Your presence will impart a stronger message than anything we can say about the importance of learning

these new skills. We would appreciate your beginning the workshop and restating the business need that prompted the workshop and what objectives you have for the training function.

7. It would be a good idea for the entire group to have lunch together. This will help us keep to the time constraints and allow the instructor to have some informal time with the participants.

## Following the Training

8. As a follow-up, give the participants a week or two to complete the development of their meeting plan.

9. Have the group meet together and ask each person to present what he or she has planned.

   — Ask the group to critique the plan and offer suggestions to ensure that the meeting will be interactive and meets the stated objectives.

   — Participants may benefit from facilitating a portion of their plan and getting feedback from the group. This is a good opportunity to try out their plan.

10. Have the group meet again after participants have been able to try out their facilitation skills. Celebrate successes, and discuss ways of handling any problems that may have arisen.

## Final Workshop Preparation

Provide a workshop registration packet of forms and essential information for each training event to the instructor or person coordinating the workshop. Consider providing a list of participants and telephone numbers or e-mail addresses so they can network following the workshop.

If the room is available, try to set up the classroom the night before the workshop. Ask the instructor to select the preferred seating arrangement based on the type of interaction used in the workshop. A variety of seating arrangements are shown on page 140, and additional suggestions for setting up the room are listed on page 141.

It may be difficult to anticipate all the needs of instructors and participants during a specific workshop. However, stocking the supplies on page 143 is a good start to creating a "survival kit" for the training room.

Arrive at least 30 to 60 minutes before the workshop begins. For last-minute issues, leave a telephone number for the instructor to reach you throughout the day.

# REGISTRATION PACKET CHECKLIST

Following is a list of items to provide to the instructor of each workshop and last-minute tasks to be completed:

_____ 1. List of participants

_____ 2. Sign-in sheet for participants

_____ 3. Blank end-of-course evaluation forms for participants to complete

_____ 4. Confirm time, date, and location of the workshop

_____ 5. Inform the instructor which materials will be delivered to the classroom or which materials have been previously sent to the instructor

_____ 6. Notify the instructor to bring any supplies not provided by you that the instructor needs to bring from his or her own supply

_____ 7. Name tents or name badges for each participant (can be preprinted or hand-lettered)

_____ 8. Certificates of completion for each participant

_____ 9. Completed pre-course Training Participant Survey responses from registered participants (see page 133 for a sample)

_____ 10. Hotel catering event order if meeting is off-site

_____ 11. List of nearby restaurants

_____ 12. Logistics and administration feedback sheet for the instructor to complete following the workshop (see page 144)

_____ 13. Names and telephone numbers of resource people who can help with last-minute issues during the day of the workshop

# ROOM SET-UP DIAGRAMS:
## SIX SUGGESTED SEATING ARRANGEMENTS

Theater

U Shape

Classroom

Conference

Chevron

Rounds

Note: Allow 2 ft. width table space per person.

# ROOM PREPARATION CHECKLIST

_____ Start with a clean room.

_____ Select the seating arrangement using the chart on the previous page based on the number of participants and the type of interaction desired.

_____ Set up audiovisual equipment (see the suggestions on the following page).

_____ Place participant materials, blank name tents, evaluation forms, pens, pencils, and other supplies on the tables.

_____ Have a sign-in sheet available.

_____ Set up a water station or place water on the participant tables.

_____ Set up refreshments.

_____ Provide trash cans.

_____ Have supplies available (see checklist on page 143).

_____ Post names and telephone numbers of resource people who are available throughout the day.

# AUDIOVISUAL HINTS

The following suggestions are for groups of fewer than 100 people. For larger groups, discuss your needs with a meeting planner at the facility you want to use.

1. The best meeting rooms for audiovisual presentations are shaped like squares with a 1:1 ratio of length to width, or like rectangles, with up to a 1:2 ratio of length to width. Be careful of odd shaped rooms or longer rectangles—it's like teaching in a bowling alley!

2. Use this ratio to identify room capacity:

   U shape with 30 in. tables     30 sq. ft. per person

   Classroom with 30 in. tables    25 sq. ft. per person

   Classroom with 18 in. tables    20 sq. ft. per person

3. Ceiling height of meeting rooms needs to be 1/6th of the length of the room. Try to get at least a 10-ft. ceiling for groups over 20 people.

4. Suggested arrangements for small groups:

   | under 20 | U shape |
   |----------|---------|
   | over 20–24 | Classroom chevron |
   | over 30 | Classroom |

5. For audiovisual projection, the screen size should be determined by the number of attendees you expect. No one should be further back than 8 times the image width. A minimum screen size of 6 ft. by 6 ft. is recommended.

6. Screen placement for educational sessions can be off-center when possible. For motivational, sales, and promotional presentations, center the screen. The instructor or presenter needs to be careful not to block the screen.

7. Legibility of projected 35-mm slides is affected by both the size of the screen and the image and the brightness of the bulb. Different zoom lenses of 4 ft. to 6 ft. can be used to fill the screen and project a larger image without changing equipment.

8. Slide quality depends on legibility. Hold a slide at arm's length against a well-lighted background. If you can read it, so can someone in the back row. Remember, no more than 8 lines of copy per slide.

9. A 19 in. color video monitor is the standard video playback unit available for rental in hotels. The viewing limit of the 19 in. monitor is 200 to 300 square feet (which is 25 to 30 people in theater style seating). Attendees numbering 200 or more are better served with video projection.

# SURVIVAL KIT FOR TRAINING ROOMS

_____ Spare projector bulbs

_____ Blank transparencies and nonpermanent marker pens

_____ Magic markers, chalk, white board markers

_____ Pens, pencils, highlighters

_____ Name tent cards (6 in. × 8 in.)

_____ Duct tape, masking tape

_____ Stapler

_____ Scissors

_____ Lined note paper, stick-on flags

_____ Extension cord, three-prong adapter

_____ Evaluation sheets

_____ Sign-in sheets

_____ Push pins

_____ Clock on instructor's table

_____ First aid kit

_____ Three-hole punch

_____ Power strip

_____ Tissues

_____ Pencil sharpener

_____ Coins for parking, phone

_____ Erasers

_____ Liquid paper

_____ Evacuation procedures

_____ Phone contact list for support personnel

_____ Return labels and box to return materials

# INSTRUCTOR FEEDBACK SHEET

Please complete this form and return it to the training department so we can better meet your needs next time.

Instructor _____ Date of Workshop _____

Classroom _____ Title of Workshop _____

Number of Participants _____

Rate the following:

| | Excellent | Good | Fair | Poor |
|---|---|---|---|---|
| Classroom ready on time | | | | |
| Materials and supplies complete and accurate for this class | | | | |
| AV in good working order | | | | |
| AV set up and ready on time | | | | |
| Enough space for the group | | | | |
| Cleanliness of room | | | | |
| Helpfulness of staff | | | | |
| Quality of food, beverages | | | | |
| Available parking | | | | |
| Information packet complete | | | | |
| Information packet received in timely manner | | | | |

General remarks about this session:

_____

_____

_____

_____

_____

## Workshop Follow-Up

After the workshop is finished, complete several essential tasks to wrap up any remaining details. Confirm that those registered actually attended the workshop and enter that information in the database that may serve as a transcript of continuing education for an employee. Complete registration information in the database for participants who were not registered. "Walk-in" participants may attend a workshop because they are last-minute substitutes for registered participants, or because they thought they were registered to attend a workshop.

Be sure to complete administrative follow-up, such as sending a certificate of completion if a participant's name was misspelled, or update information in the database. Use the checklist on page 146 to identify recommended tasks.

Discuss with your training manager what type of statistics to use to track training results in your organization. Often commercial software programs encourage entering evaluation comments in the database to track training results. See Chapter 15 for suggestions for creating a trend analysis for specific workshops.

# WORKSHOP FOLLOW-UP CHECKLIST

*(Use this checklist to close out completed workshops.)*

_____ Review the workshop evaluation sheets and enter participant ratings and written comments into the registration software. Create a summary for the workshop. See Chapter 15 for suggestions on creating a trend analysis from summary information.

_____ Address issues raised by participants on evaluation forms in a timely manner.

_____ Confirm which participants attended training as well as who was registered but did not attend training, and who attended and was not registered.

_____ Update and/or make changes in participant information in the database (name, address, telephone, e-mail address, etc.).

_____ Address issues raised by the instructor from the Instructor Feedback Sheet. File the sheet for future reference.

_____ Send certificates of completion for "walk-in" and substitute participants.

_____ Restore unused supplies and workshop materials.

Chapter 12

# How to Set Up Off-Site Training Events

## Objectives

- Negotiate with hotels for off-site meeting rooms.
- Coordinate off-site facility arrangements.
- Make travel arrangements for instructors and training participants.

## Chapter Tools

- Off-site Meeting Planning Checklist
- Sample Workshop Room and Service Requirments
- Hotel Evaluation
- Travel Agency Expectations
- Personal Traveler Profile

## Questions

Use these questions to identify your current development level for the issues addressed in this chapter.

1. *Which stage of development describes how your training department selects and deals with off-site training facilities for specific training events?*

   — Stage 1: No outside facilities are used.

   — Stage 2: Outside facilities are used on an as needed basis without an established system.

   — Stage 3: Requirements for off-site facilities are clearly communicated, and at least two facilities are contacted for competitive bids.

   — Stage 4: Requirements are systematically met by one or two off-site facilities with regular feedback provided to keep service at a highly satisfactory level.

   — Stage 5: We partner with off-site facilities to meet a variety of needs and have a continuous improvement process in place.

2. *Which stage of development describes how your training department makes travel arrangements for instructors and participants.*

   — Stage 1: The training department makes no travel arrangements. Instructors and participants make their own travel arrangements.

   — Stage 2: The corporate travel department—or an external travel agent—makes arrangements as needed for instructors and participants.

   — Stage 3: The training department recommends specific hotels, airlines, and rental car companies with which corporate rates have been negotiated.

   — Stage 4: The training department makes or coordinates, with the travel agent, hotel, car rental, and air travel reservations from preferences identified in the traveler's profile.

   — Stage 5: The training department makes or coordinates, with the travel agent, all travel arrangements, including ground transfers and airport pickup service, and constantly strives to improve the level of service.

If you rated yourself at Stage 1 or Stage 2 for most of these diagnostic questions, you might want to proceed through this chapter as it is written. If you rated yourself at Stage 3 or higher, you might benefit from previewing the tools provided in this chapter before working through the ideas and suggestions provided with the checklists.

## Negotiating with Hotels

Before negotiating with hotels to conduct a training event at an off-site training facility, write down your facility and service needs. It is much easier to deal with the hotel's meeting planners if you are clear about what you want. Many of the checklists in Chapter 11 can be modified to use to plan an off-site training event. Use the checklist on page 150 to identify the different types of facilities and services you want from an off-site facility.

After creating a checklist of rooms and services needed for an off-site training meeting, write your requests in a format that helps the hotel meet your needs. A suggested sample requirement description can be found on page 151. Different hotel staff have different functions. "Sales" staff work with guests who require sleeping rooms along with banquet facilities. "Catering" staff work with guests who use banquet facilities but do not require sleeping rooms. "Banquet" staff directly assist guests on the day of the event. A banquet captain or supervisor is usually assigned to a group of meeting rooms. Each room usually has a specific server or food service staff. If the meeting room is not set up as you requested, the banquet staff can usually help make setup changes. Some hotels have different staff set up the meeting rooms. If you change the setup of the meeting room after it has been set up according to the original request, there can be a charge to reset the room.

When negotiating with off-site facilities, remember that many of the regular rates for facilities and services are negotiable. Getting a better price on facilities and services often depends on how many meeting rooms are booked for a single event or for a period of a year. For example, it is typical of most hotels that room rental is waived when a full meal is served. A full meal is a served breakfast or a served buffet luncheon or dinner.

Meal pricing is usually per person. Identify all the courses and which types of beverages are included in the price. Most prices are quoted without local taxes or gratuity. Most hotels charge a fixed gratuity amount that ranges from 15 to 20 percent, depending on the type of services requested.

Establish the method of payment prior to signing a formal agreement. Most hotels extend credit to corporate accounts after a credit application is completed. New customers are often asked to provide a deposit equal to the amount of room rent.

Get information on the hotel's cancellation policy. Once a contract is signed, the organization becomes obligated to adhere to the terms of the agreement. Some contracts require full payment of all expected revenue if the event is canceled. Some facilities allow cancellation without paying a penalty when the cancellation is made 30 to 60 days prior to the event.

Ask the hotel whether you may bring your own equipment to its facility. Hotels usually permit using your own equipment but rarely permit outside food and beverages.

Identify the hotel's policy on taping or tacking paper or decorations on the walls. Most hotels allow masking tape; however, some are very restrictive and allow no taping or pins of any type.

Inquire about the hotel's security policy. For groups of more than 100 people, the hotel may require some type of security arrangement for the event. Find out when the room will be locked and what type of materials and/or equipment the hotel will be responsible for if stolen from a locked room.

Typically, when an event is booked, the hotel asks the customer to identify the expected number of participants. The hotel assigns the appropriate size room and plans for meal service based on this estimate. Hotels often charge a penalty if the actual number of guests drops below the expected number. Read the fine print on the hotel's Banquet Event Order. Hotels usually ask for a guaranteed number of participants 72 hours prior to the event. The hotel will serve an agreed-upon percentage of people over the "set for" number of participants. To avoid paying for food and service for "no show" participants, it is wise to guarantee somewhat fewer participants (allowed in your contract) than the "set for" number.

# OFF-SITE MEETING PLANNING CHECKLIST

*(Check the items the off-site facility needs to provide.)*

_____ Number of meeting rooms

_____ Date, times (start, end, breaks)

_____ Size of rooms for the number of participants (20–30 sq. ft. per person)

_____ Room setup (see page 140)

_____ Audiovisual requirements (see page 142)

_____ Refreshments, water

_____ Number of meals to serve

_____ Number of sleeping rooms

_____ Any VIP arrangements

_____ What is the hotel's policy on cancellations

_____ Handicapped access (ADA compliance)

_____ Parking, parking validation

_____ Accessibility to electric outlets

_____ Coat rack

_____ Trash cans and wastebaskets

_____ Directions to public transportation, shuttle service

_____ Security for equipment

_____ Person to accept shipped materials

# SAMPLE WORKSHOP ROOM AND
# SERVICE REQUIREMENTS

*(Provide your requirements in writing to the off-site facility.)*

## Meeting Room

We require a quiet, well-ventilated room that can comfortably hold ___ (fill in the number) participants in a classroom style seating arrangement (at tables and chairs) if 21 or more attend. If 20 or less attend, we require a "U" shape seating arrangement with chairs on the outside of the "U" only [or specify type of seating arrangement].

All tables should have tablecloths and, if the seating arrangement is in a "U" shape, also provide draping. Water and glasses should be on the tables and *NO* ashtrays should be in the room. Several should be available *outside* the room or wherever smoking is allowed in your facility. The room should be set up by 8:00 am the morning of the seminar. If possible, the room should be set up the night before.

Place a 6-foot draped head table at the front of the room for the speaker (attach a diagram from page 140). Place a small table outside the room, near the door for registrations. Place an 8-foot draped table in the rear of the room for a book display.

## Equipment

This seminar requires the following equipment (audiovisual and other):

[list equipment]

The equipment must be available by 8:00 am the morning of the workshop. The equipment may be picked up after 5:00 pm the same day. Of course, it's critical that the equipment is in excellent working order and spare bulbs are available for any projectors ordered.

## Beverage Service

At 8:00 am and 10:15 am on the day of the workshop, set up a coffee service inside the classroom containing regular coffee, brewed decaffeinated coffee, and hot water and tea bags. Provide the usual condiments of cream, sugar, lemon, etc.

At 2:15 pm, provide a cold drink service consisting of half diet and half regular sodas set up in the rear of the meeting room.

We will vacate the room by 5:00 pm.

# HOTEL EVALUATION

*(Instructor completes this form following an off-site training event.)*

Instructor: _____   Date of Workshop: _____

Hotel: _____   City: _____

Meeting Room: _____   # of Participants: _____

Rate the following:

|                                    | Excellent | Good | Fair | Poor |
|------------------------------------|-----------|------|------|------|
| Room ready on time                 | _____     | _____ | _____ | _____ |
| AV in good working order           | _____     | _____ | _____ | _____ |
| AV set up and ready on time        | _____     | _____ | _____ | _____ |
| Enough space for your group        | _____     | _____ | _____ | _____ |
| Cleanliness of room                | _____     | _____ | _____ | _____ |
| Helpfulness of staff               | _____     | _____ | _____ | _____ |
| Sleeping room: clean               | _____     | _____ | _____ | _____ |
| Sleeping room: attractive          | _____     | _____ | _____ | _____ |
| Availability of restaurants        | _____     | _____ | _____ | _____ |
| Availability of parking and rate   | _____     | _____ | _____ | _____ |

Would you suggest using this hotel for future meetings?

_____ Yes

_____ Only if nothing else is available

_____ Definitely not!

Suggestions or Comments:

## Travel Arrangements

When making travel arrangements with an internal travel department or external travel agent, identify the type of services and level of service you expect. The checklist on the following page will help you set expectations based on the needs of your training organization.

When making and/or coordinating travel arrangements for instructors and others, use or customize the traveler profile on page 155.

# TRAVEL AGENCY EXPECTATIONS

*(Share these expectations with those making reservations.)*

_____ Willing to find the best air and car rental service, routing, and itineraries at the lowest cost.

_____ Agency staff are available five days a week during normal business hours.

_____ Provides 24-hour emergency service.

_____ Can deliver tickets to the traveler at least three days prior to departure or provide "E" tickets via fax on the same day.

_____ Can consistently provide the same two or three travel agents to service this account and are willing to get to know our instructors and their travel preferences.

_____ Is willing to quote the cost of an itinerary within 24 hours or sooner.

_____ Can get upgrades and perks available only through full-service travel agencies.

# PERSONAL TRAVELER PROFILE

*(To be completed by each person served by the training department or travel agent.)*

Name _____  Title _____

Department _____  Telephone _____

Company _____

Office address _____

Residence address _____

Home telephone _____  E-mail _____

Passport number _____  Expiration date _____

Where was this passport issued? _____

Disabilities requiring special accommodation: _____

## Airline Travel

Class of service preference: _____

Seating preference: _____

Special meal requirements: _____

## Airline Club Memberships and Numbers

Airline _____  # _____

Airline _____  # _____

Airline _____  # _____

## Hotel Memberships and Numbers

Hotel _____  # _____

Hotel _____  # _____

Hotel _____  # _____

Special hotel accommodation: _____

___ smoking room, ___ nonsmoking room

___ suite, ___ junior suite, ___ king bed, ___ queen bed, ___ twin beds

___ Guarantee for late arrival? If so, credit card # _____

Expiration date of credit card _____

___ Visa, ___ MasterCard, ___ American Express, ____ Discover, ____ Diner's Club

## Rental Car Memberships and Numbers

Car company _____ # _____

Car company _____ # _____

Car company _____ # _____

Size of rental car: ___ sub-compact, ___ compact, ___ mid-size, ___ full-size

## Ground Transportation Requirements

___ Wants bus, taxi, shuttle, or other means to reach hotel

___ Needs reservation for car service to meet at airport and transport to hotel

___ Needs driving directions to hotel

## Chapter 13

# Set Up and Run a Corporate Resource Center

## Objectives

- Maintain a corporate library and/or resource center with up-to-date information.

- Purchase audiovisual equipment.

- Handle maintenance functions with ease.

- Duplicate and inventory training materials.

- Order training supplies.

- Produce audiovisual and written materials.

- Set a standard (style guide) for printed training materials.

- Monitor tuition reimbursement programs.

## Chapter Tools

- Corporate Library and Resource Center Checklist

- Equipment Purchase Checklist

- Maintenance Inventory Template

- Equipment Inventory Template

- Training Materials Inventory

- Supply Order Template

- Tuition Reimbursement Form

## Questions

Use these questions to identify your current development level for the issues addressed in this chapter.

1. *Which stage of development describes how your training function selects and maintains audiovisual equipment?*

   — Stage 1: No clear criteria exist for the selection of audiovisual equipment.

   — Stage 2: Selection criteria are clear. Proposals are requested to compare similar equipment. References are checked.

   — Stage 3: Equipment specifications are written, and proposals are reviewed with input from internal clients.

   — Stage 4: A systematic process exists for gathering resources and reviewing and selecting training equipment, with input from internal clients, against written criteria. Shared use of equipment is encouraged where appropriate.

   — Stage 5: A systematic process exists for gathering resources and reviewing and selecting training equipment, with input from internal clients, against written criteria. Shared use of equipment is encouraged where appropriate. Each request for a new piece of equipment is matched with the changing needs of the organization.

2. *Which stage of development describes how your training department provides support services and acts as a resource center for the organization?*

   — Stage 1: No additional support services are offered.

   — Stage 2: Specific guidelines from trainers and participants are met on a limited basis.

   — Stage 3: A specialist is available to develop color transparencies, custom graphics, PowerPoint presentations, etc. Guidelines exist to access resources provided by the training department.

   — Stage 4: Specialized requests, based on individual needs of trainers or management, are systematically met.

   — Stage 5: Specialized services are tailored to meet the needs of target groups and clients.

If you rated yourself at Stage 1 or Stage 2 for most of these diagnostic questions, you might want to proceed through this chapter as it is written. If you rated yourself at Stage 3 or higher, you might benefit from previewing the tools provided in this chapter before working through the ideas and suggestions provided with the checklists.

## Corporate Library and Resource Center

Resources for learning and development should be centralized in the training department. Systematically organize and publicize the resource center's inventory of equipment, videotapes, and services to promote access and use by employees. See a suggested checklist of equipment, services, and resources on page 160.

Key Issues to consider when setting up this type of resource center include

1. Select a central location to house the materials. Identify who in the training department will staff the resource center and be responsible for its function and inventory. A conference room, storage room, and access for employees are important considerations in selecting a site.

2. Establish a checkout system to control the return of loaned materials. Create a log and identify equipment by an inventory number. Tell the borrower when the item needs to be returned.

3. Establish a method and source of funding for keeping materials up to date and relevant to the organization.

4. Regularly report to management the usefulness of the equipment and services and how the organization is experiencing a return on its investment in the materials provided by the resource center.

# CORPORATE LIBRARY AND
# RESOURCE CENTER CHECKLIST

*(Suggestions for information and services to provide to your organization through a corporate library or resource center.)*

**Equipment available**

- Projectors

- Easels

- Video camera and recorder

- Audio cassette

- Personal computer

**Services**

- Collect information on conferences and external training programs

- Lend, service, and maintain equipment

- Overhead transparency development and production

- 35 mm slide production

- Ordering special products or equipment for management or training

- Periodical clipping service

- Indexing and listing of departmental or personal collections of books and periodicals

**On loan**

- Film and video library

- Periodicals and journals; books

- Personal computer software

**Subject areas for consideration (collect information on)**

- Your industry

- Your company's history

- Federal and state legislation

- Human resource development

- Career development

- Personal development

- Professional associations

## Purchase Audiovisual Equipment

When purchasing audiovisual equipment, having a clear idea of your requirements can save money, disappointment, and buyer's remorse. First consider the needs of the equipment users. Identify the location where the equipment will be used. If video equipment is part of the organization's training programs, a classroom larger than 400 square feet will need more than one monitor so all participants can see the screen. Consider video projection equipment that can also project images from a laptop computer.

Discuss equipment needs in addition to size and location needs with the instructors who will use the classroom. Consider how often equipment will be used. Equipment with high-volume use should be durable and dependable and require minimum maintenance.

Once you've identified your needs for different types of equipment, solicit competitive bids from at least three suppliers. Be careful to compare equipment with similar features so cost figures are not distorted by unnecessary add-on features. See the equipment checklist on the following page for items to consider when buying audiovisual equipment.

## Equipment Maintenance and Inventory

Even the "mechanically challenged" can keep track of the need to maintain the various equipment in the training department. Use the Maintenance Inventory Template on page 163 to keep track of what equipment belongs to the department, when it was purchased, when the warranty expires, when to conduct preventive maintenance, storage requirements, and replacement part numbers (bulbs, batteries, etc.).

Use the Equipment Inventory Template form on page 164 to keep track of equipment and furnishings owned by the training department.

# EQUIPMENT PURCHASE CHECKLIST

*(Review the items below prior to purchasing equipment.)*

_____ Describe the business need related to this equipment purchase.

_____ Identify how many times per year or month this equipment may be used.

_____ What are the physical limits of the room where the equipment is to be used?

_____ If a projector is to be purchased, what is the typical audience size?

_____ What are the main features this equipment needs to have?

_____ What are optional features that are desirable, such as a wireless remote.

_____ Identify at least three sources for this equipment.

_____ Write a description of your objectives and intended use for this equipment.

_____ Share the description with suppliers and ask for product information to meet the needs.

_____ Review product information and identify at least three pieces of equipment that could meet your requirements.

_____ Review warranty information, maintenance recommendations, and other specifications.

_____ Ask the vendor for references for satisfied customers now using this equipment.

_____ Schedule a product demonstration and ask the vendor for a written proposal if the cost exceeds your buying limit.

_____ Recommend purchase of a specific piece of equipment and get approvals.

_____ Follow the purchasing process required in your organization.

# MAINTENANCE INVENTORY TEMPLATE

*(Use this template to inventory and schedule maintenance for department equipment.)*

| Equipment Description | Serial Number | Date Purchased | Warranty Expiration Date | Enter Date of Maintenance | | | | | Part Numbers (batteries/bulbs) |
|---|---|---|---|---|---|---|---|---|---|
| | | | | | | | | | |
| | | | | | | | | | |
| | | | | | | | | | |
| | | | | | | | | | |
| | | | | | | | | | |
| | | | | | | | | | |
| | | | | | | | | | |
| | | | | | | | | | |
| | | | | | | | | | |
| | | | | | | | | | |
| | | | | | | | | | |
| | | | | | | | | | |
| | | | | | | | | | |
| | | | | | | | | | |
| | | | | | | | | | |
| | | | | | | | | | |
| | | | | | | | | | |
| | | | | | | | | | |
| | | | | | | | | | |

# EQUIPMENT INVENTORY TEMPLATE

*(Use this template to inventory department equipment.)*

| Equipment Description | Model Number | Serial Number | Date Purchased | Responsible Person/Owner | Room Location | Part Numbers (batteries/bulbs) |
|---|---|---|---|---|---|---|
| | | | | | | |
| | | | | | | |
| | | | | | | |
| | | | | | | |
| | | | | | | |
| | | | | | | |
| | | | | | | |
| | | | | | | |
| | | | | | | |
| | | | | | | |
| | | | | | | |
| | | | | | | |
| | | | | | | |
| | | | | | | |
| | | | | | | |
| | | | | | | |
| | | | | | | |
| | | | | | | |
| | | | | | | |
| | | | | | | |

## Training Materials Inventory and Ordering

For each workshop the training department presents, identify the expected number of participants and decide how many sets of handout materials or participant manuals to print. Check with the course designer or instructor to identify what materials and supplies are needed. Printing 10 percent more than the number required will save last-minute rush orders if class size increases through last-minute registrations. When initiating print orders, plan to have all materials printed and delivered to the workshop site two weeks prior to the training event. If materials do not reach their intended destination, there is still time to reprint materials or otherwise troubleshoot the problem. For distance learning situations, try sending hard or electronic copy to the site coordinator at least one month ahead of the scheduled training program along with duplication instructions.

Use the template on the next page to keep track of how many sets of materials are needed. Also, consider "print on demand" systems. Some organizations provide all their materials through the organization's intranet and recommend that employees download the required materials to their computer and print them for a specific training session.

Use the suggested list of supplies for the training department on page 167 as a template for ordering needed supplies for a period of time. Once you decide what supply you need on hand, that number becomes the "par" or what level of supply to maintain. Decide what quantity will be the "order point" and what quantity will be ordered at that point. Take inventory at least monthly, depending on how rapidly supplies are used.

# TRAINING MATERIALS INVENTORY

*(Use this form to inventory and reorder training materials.)*

| Course Title | Estimated Number of Participants | Date of Workshop | Date Materials Sent to Printer | Date Materials Back from Printer | Location of Workshop | Date Materials Shipped | Number of Sets of Materials Shipped | Person Responsible at Training Site | Verify Materials Arrived |
|---|---|---|---|---|---|---|---|---|---|
| | | | | | | | | | |
| | | | | | | | | | |
| | | | | | | | | | |
| | | | | | | | | | |
| | | | | | | | | | |
| | | | | | | | | | |
| | | | | | | | | | |
| | | | | | | | | | |
| | | | | | | | | | |
| | | | | | | | | | |
| | | | | | | | | | |
| | | | | | | | | | |
| | | | | | | | | | |
| | | | | | | | | | |
| | | | | | | | | | |
| | | | | | | | | | |
| | | | | | | | | | |

# SUPPLY ORDER TEMPLATE

*(Use this template to take inventory and reorder training supplies.)*

| Supply Item | Par | Order Point | Order Quantity | Date Ordered | Date Received |
|---|---|---|---|---|---|
| Projector bulbs | | | | | |
| Batteries for remotes | | | | | |
| Erasable transparency pens | | | | | |
| Color transparency film | | | | | |
| Blank transparencies | | | | | |
| Permanent magic markers | | | | | |
| White board markers | | | | | |
| White board eraser | | | | | |
| Chalk | | | | | |
| Chalkboard eraser | | | | | |
| Name tent cards | | | | | |
| Duct tape | | | | | |
| Masking tape | | | | | |
| Push pins | | | | | |
| Pencil sharpener | | | | | |
| Lined note paper | | | | | |
| Pencils | | | | | |
| Pens | | | | | |
| Highlighters | | | | | |

## Produce Audiovisual and Written Materials

The training department can provide a resource to the organization by producing a variety of materials for internal presentations and training programs. First, work with a graphic designer to determine what standards all employees who develop training and presentation materials will use. Publish those standards along with examples and templates on the company's intranet. When creating a style guide, consider the following points:

- Preferred font and point size for type

- Margins and spacing

- Headers and footers

- Location of date, author, title on the page

- Use of corporate logo

- Type and color of paper

- Type of binding

- One-sided or two-sided copying

- Page numbering system

When producing electronic presentations and/or overhead transparencies, make similar decisions about the appearance of graphics used in presentations. Consider these points:

- Use of color

- Preferred fonts and point size

- Headers and footers

- Amount of copy on a page

- Recommended amount of animation

## Tuition Reimbursement Programs

Many training departments provide resources for attending outside workshops, seminars, and college and university degree and certificate programs. When developing this type of program, consider these points:

- How are employees selected and approved to attend outside programs?

- Following attendance at a workshop, does the employee submit an expense report and a certificate of completion for reimbursement through his or her department?

- Have the employee complete an evaluation of the program to assist in selection of future programs.

- Give the training department copies of the evaluation and the certificate for the employee's transcript.

- Have the employee report to the supervisor and/or department members what he or she has learned and how this knowledge can be applied in the employee's work setting.

- Provide employees with clear instructions on how to request reimbursement of their expenses.

Use the form on the next page for employees who request reimbursement of outside training expenses.

# TUITION REIMBURSEMENT FORM

Employee's Name: _____

Job title: _____ Supervisor: _____

Title of course: _____

Vendor/School: _____

Location of course: _____

Number of hours: _____

Report given to supervisor or department describing what knowledge was gained that will benefit the

organization: _____ (date)

Recommend this course to others: ____ highly ___ somewhat ___ not recommended

Cost of course: _____ Cost of materials: _____

Cost of travel: _____

Amount of reimbursement requested: _____

Grade received: _____ enter letter grade or pass/fail and attach a copy of transcript

____ Attach a copy of the certificate of completion

Employee's Signature: _____ Date: _____

═══════════════════════════════════════════════════════

Approvals:

Print name of employee's supervisor _____

Supervisor's signature _____ Date: _____

Finance department approval by: _____

Finance department signature: _____ Date: _____

Check number: _____ Amount: _____ Date issued: _____

## Chapter 14

# Show Me the Money:
# Budgeting for Training

## Objectives

- Perform feasibility analysis—is training worth it?

- Identify the cost of training.

- Prepare and monitor the training budget.

- Maintain vital statistics of the training function.

- Identify valuable statistics about the events and performance for training in your organization.

- Participate in budgeting decisions.

## Chapter Tools

- Feasibility Analysis Template

- Cost of Training Template

- Training Budget Template and Worksheet

- Resource Requirements Worksheet

## Question

Use this question to identify your current development level for the issues addressed in this chapter.

1. *Which stage of development describes how your training function identifies the feasibility of conducting training?*

   — Stage 1: No feasibility analysis is done.

   — Stage 2: An estimate of training costs is created prior to each training event.

   — Stage 3: A budget is developed that identifies the cost of training and the benefits expected from conducting the training.

   — Stage 4: A training budget is created systematically. Unanticipated training events require a feasibility analysis prior to approval.

   — Stage 5: Statistics are used to demonstrate the results of training, are compared with the feasibility analysis, and are a regular part of the budgeting process.

If you rated yourself at Stage 1 or Stage 2 for this diagnostic question, you might want to proceed through this chapter as it is written. If you rated yourself at Stage 3 or higher, you might benefit from previewing the tools provided in this chapter before working through the ideas and suggestions provided with the checklists.

## Feasibility Analysis

A feasibility analysis compares the cost of conducting training to the cost of not conducting training to determine whether the training is worth doing. It may be that the cost of providing a remedy to a problem that involves training may be either too expensive as a solution to respond to a minor issue or not worth the effort compared with the current situation.

First, identify the current cost of doing nothing about the issue in question. The Feasibility Analysis Template on page 174 suggests some costs to assess. Next, identify the cost associated with providing the training. See the Cost of Training template on page 175 for some of these costs. Compare the two costs. If the cost of doing the training is less than the cost of doing no training, it may be feasible to do the training to eliminate or reduce the costs of continuing the current method of doing business.

## Cost of Training

Consider listing three types of costs for designing and conducting a training program. First, identify direct costs. These are costs associated directly with conducting a specific training program. What is the cost to design this program, calculated either in terms of the salary of an internal employee or the fee of an external person? What is the cost of an internal instructor or external instructor to conduct each session of this training? What travel and overnight expenses do the instructor and employees incur to attend this training? What are the classroom rent, meals, and refreshment costs incurred to conduct each session of this training?

Second, what are the indirect costs assigned to this training program? To identify indirect costs, identify all overhead along with general and administrative costs incurred by the training department in a year—for example, the cost of office space, utilities, and administrative support not associated with any specific training program. Total these costs and divide by the number of training events occurring during the year. Assign a portion of the indirect or overhead costs to each workshop session.

Third, identify the compensation of participants attending training. It is appropriate to include employee compensation as a cost of training if the employees attending training are either revenue producers or need to be replaced by a substitute to attend training. Sales revenue is lost and there is a cost of a replacement employee in a 24-hour operation. To reflect an accurate cost of training, include either the cost of lost revenue, the cost of the replacement person, or the salary of the employee in the cost of training. If there is no lost sales revenue or replacement required for an employee to attend training, the participant's salary is generally not included in the cost of training.

## Training Budget Worksheet

To use the Cost of Training template as a budget worksheet, show estimated and actual columns in the Cost of Training template as shown on page 176. A training budget needs to be monitored on at least a monthly basis.

# FEASIBILITY ANALYSIS TEMPLATE

*(Use this template to decide if the result of training is greater than the cost of doing the training.)*

Describe the issue that may be totally or partially remedied by providing training:

Identify the cost of doing nothing by estimating

_____ Lost Time (cost of salary per hour)

_____ Lost Revenue or Sales (what is the cost)

_____ Inefficient Work Flow (cost of salary per hour of those involved)

_____ Waiting Time (salary per hour of those who wait)

_____ Poor Product Quality (loss of increased sales for an improved product)

_____ Miscommunication (amount spent on mistakes and remedies)

_____ Poor Appearance of Service Workers (amount of added sales lost)

_____ Misused Supplies (cost of supplies)

_____ Customer Complaint (cost to fix current complaints)

_____ Poor Safety (losses in employee time, medical expenses, high premiums)

_____ Poor Job Satisfaction (cost of turnover, abused sick leave)

_____ Slow Service (salary per hour of those who wait for service)

_____ Repetitious Process (current cost of duplicate work)

_____ Theft (cost of losses)

_____ Total cost of current situation

Compare the total cost above to the cost of training established by using the template on the next page. If the cost of training is less, it may be worth doing.

# COST OF TRAINING TEMPLATE

*(Identify the cost to design and conduct a training program.)*

**Direct costs**

_____ Course design

_____ Instructor fee or salary for hours to prepare and conduct training

_____ Produce audiovisual materials

_____ Travel and overnight expense for instructor

_____ Travel and overnight expenses for employees attending training

_____ Meals and refreshments served at training program

_____ Classroom rent

_____ Total (Direct costs)


**Indirect costs (overhead)**

_____ Subtotal of direct and indirect costs

_____ Participant compensation

_____ Total costs

# TRAINING BUDGET TEMPLATE AND WORKSHEET

*(Identify the estimated and actual costs to design and conduct a training program.)*

| Estimated Cost | Actual Cost |
|---|---|

**Direct costs**

| | | |
|---|---|---|
| _____ | _____ | Course design |
| _____ | _____ | Instructor fee or salary for hours to prepare and conduct training |
| _____ | _____ | Produce audiovisual materials |
| _____ | _____ | Travel and overnight expense for instructor |
| _____ | _____ | Travel and overnight expenses for employees attending training |
| _____ | _____ | Meals and refreshments served at training program |
| _____ | _____ | Classroom rent |
| _____ | _____ | Total (Direct costs) |

**Indirect costs (overhead)**

| | | |
|---|---|---|
| _____ | _____ | Subtotal of direct and indirect costs |
| _____ | _____ | Participant compensation |
| _____ | _____ | Total costs |

## Resource Requirements

When developing a training program, compare the cost of delivering training through different mediums. For example, if you have a group of 150 employees to train in three locations, will you get a better result if (1) the same trainer conducts several training sessions in three locations, (2) you use a self-paced or distance learning option, or (3) trainers at three locations deliver sessions on an as needed basis?

To help decide which training delivery medium is best for a given workshop, consider the resources required to assess, design, develop, deliver, and evaluate the training using each of the considered mediums. Use the Resource Requirements Worksheets on page 178–179 to identify various cost advantages and disadvantages. Consider three additional factors in selecting different mediums for training delivery, expertise, and uniformity of information delivered. First, if time is a critical factor, consider how long it will take to assess, design, develop, deliver, and evaluate the training using each of the options under consideration. For example, internal subject matter experts may have expertise and could consistently deliver a quality message, but may not be able to afford time away from their regular duties.

Second, consider whether each of the media has expertise and experience in the topic of the workshop. For example, internal subject matter experts may have the expertise to deliver training, but may not have the required skills to assess training needs or develop training materials.

Third, does the information delivered need to be thoroughly consistent from one session to another and, if so, which medium is the best option to provide consistency. For example, if a new performance appraisal system is being rolled out and each employee needs to hear a consistent policy, tone, and message, then having a few trainers, instead of several, will provide greater consistency.

# RESOURCE REQUIREMENTS WORKSHEET

*(Enter cost figures for each delivery option.)*

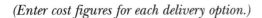
| Type of cost:<br><br>Customize the delivery options at the right and cost each of these options during four stages of design and delivery of training. | Centralized Delivery | Decentralized Delivery | Distance Learning | Package Program | Self-Paced | External Resource |
|---|---|---|---|---|---|---|
| Time of people conducting needs assessment | | | | | | |
| Equipment and materials used to conduct needs assessment | | | | | | |
| Facility cost | | | | | | |
| Total assessment costs | | | | | | |
| | | | | | | |
| Time of people to design and develop training materials, leaders guide, visual and job aids | | | | | | |
| Equipment and materials used to design and develop materials | | | | | | |
| Facility cost to develop materials | | | | | | |
| Total design and development costs | | | | | | |
| | | | | | | |
| Time and people to deliver training | | | | | | |
| Equipment and materials used to deliver training | | | | | | |
| Facility cost to deliver training | | | | | | |
| Travel costs to deliver training | | | | | | |
| Total training delivery costs | | | | | | |
| | | | | | | |
| Time and people to evaluate training | | | | | | |
| Equipment and materials to evaluate training | | | | | | |
| Facility cost to evaluate training | | | | | | |
| Total training evaluation costs | | | | | | |
| | | | | | | |
| Total of all costs for each medium | | | | | | |

| For the three questions below use this rating scale:<br><br>1 = poor, few requirements met<br><br>3 = some requirements met<br><br>5 = excellent, almost all requirements met | | | | | | |
|---|---|---|---|---|---|---|
| Which option can deliver training within the required time frame? | | | | | | |
| Which option offers the best expertise and experience for this training? | | | | | | |
| Which option will deliver the same message at each training session? | | | | | | |
| Which option is the best learning method for the learning objectives and materials used during training? | | | | | | |
| Total points for each option: | | | | | | |

Given cost comparison and other factors, which of the delivery options is best to meet the needs of this training?

## Vital Statistics of the Training Function

Compile performance statistics on a regular basis to demonstrate results and performance. Regularly measure the following:

- Cost of conducting a specific training program

- Percent of payroll spent on training, organizationwide

- Cost benefit analysis showing results of training (see Chapter 15)

- Number of employees attending each session of training

- Class size for each training session

- Average class size for a series of workshop sessions for the same program

- Number of instruction hours for the department

- Number of instruction hours per trainer

- Number of training hours per employee per year

- Number of hours for instructors to prepare for training sessions

- Number of hours spent in instructor travel

- Expense of marketing training programs

- Cost of continuing education for trainers

- Amount of time trainers spend in continuing education (total and per person)

- Cost of training materials (total and per person)

- Cost of inventory (equipment and materials)

In addition, consider reporting trends and results of training on a regular basis to management and internal customers. Statistics are easier to read and interpret when presented in graphic form. The way to be included in decision making is to provide information on a regular basis.

## Chapter 15

# How to Evaluate and Demonstrate the Success of Training

## Objectives

- Establish criteria to measure the results of training.

- Evaluate the effectiveness of training done in your organization.

- Gauge customer satisfaction and perform trend analysis.

- Measure results.

## Chapter Tools

- Sample Participant Reaction Sheet

- Cost-Benefit Analysis Example

- Cost-Benefit Analysis

## Questions

Use these questions to identify your current development level for the issues addressed in this chapter.

1. *Which stage of development describes how your training department evaluates participant reactions to training events?*

   — Stage 1: No formal evaluation is performed, or the instructor performs evaluation only informally.

   — Stage 2: A checklist with ratings asks for participants' reactions, level of satisfaction with the content, and skill of the instructor.

   — Stage 3: A summary report is created from participants' reactions and provided to the instructor and the internal customer.

   — Stage 4: A summary report is shared with the instructor, the internal customer, and the course designer to systematically improve the content and process of instruction.

   — Stage 5: Trend analysis incorporates summary information to continuously improve the content and process of instruction.

2. *Which stage of development describes how the results of training are measured?*

   — Stage 1: No results are measured.

   — Stage 2: No results are measured, but instructors or supervisors may collect informal information about the results of training.

   — Stage 3: The trainer and/or supervisor identifies the costs associated with the development and delivery of training.

   — Stage 4: The trainer and/or supervisor creates a cost-benefit analysis to identify the bottom line impact and how well training met the business need associated with each course. The training department measures training outcomes against the training plan.

   — Stage 5: The training department relates the cost-benefit analysis to the business need, and revises the training plan as appropriate with input from the client.

If you rated yourself at Stage 1 or Stage 2 for this diagnostic question, you might want to proceed through this chapter as it is written. If you rated yourself at Stage 3 or higher, you might benefit from previewing the tools provided in this chapter before working through the ideas and suggestions provided with the checklists.

Donald Kirkpatrick first identified the four levels of evaluation and outlined information about each level of evaluation in his book, *Evaluating Training Programs: The Four Levels.* Since this book is about the administration of training events *outside* the classroom, only Level one (reaction of participants to training events) and Level four (measure the bottom line results of training) are addressed here.

## Evaluate Participant Reactions to Training

Use Level I evaluation to identify the effectiveness of a training program. Both the learners and the instructor tell the course designer what was effective and what needed improvement. Participants are asked to comment on the course materials, instructor effectiveness, and training environment and provide an overall rating for a course. A sample reaction sheet appears on pages 184–185.

The top of the form asks for the participant's name. In general, participants are likely to provide more complete information if their names are attached to the information. However, participants who choose to remain anonymous can leave this blank. The second piece of information requested is the reason the participant attends the workshop. There seems to be a correlation between self-nomination and the value of the workshop to a participant. The reasons for attending can help you interpret general comments and the participant's reaction to the workshop.

Asking for the participant's years of experience can help the course developer weight the comments appropriately to determine how well the participant matches the target population for whom the course is designed. For example, the trend analysis information on page 186 analyzes participant comments from a course with a target population of trainers with less than one year of experience. Some participants with five or more years of experience understandably said that the workshop was too basic.

The next four questions deal with what was most and least beneficial along with what content needs to be added or deleted. The type of response requested is not a check mark or a rating, but short answers to be written by the participant. Give the participant a combination of short answer and rating comments to ease the completion of the form.

The bottom of the first page asks for a rating, on a scale of 1 to 7, of the instructor's skills and information; about the design of visuals, activities, and exercises; and about the value of the handout book for future reference. The scale of 1 to 7 is preferred over a 10-point scale to avoid comparison to other grading systems (e.g., 90 percent = A) that are familiar to the participants. The more specifically worded the rated element, the more likely instructors are to pay attention to that element.

The second page of the evaluation form asks for an opinion about the workshop using a four-point scale. The first question gives the option of "this is my first workshop" in the event there is no point of comparison. Using these three questions allows a point of comparison and the ability to establish a company standard of performance. Use these three questions as the basis for a trend analysis to compare the success of one training program with another, or against a standard. See the trend analysis section of this chapter for more information.

The next question asks whether the content of the course is customized appropriately to meet the needs of this organization. Answers to this question are helpful to the course designer.

Asking for the name of the person who approved attendance at this workshop helps the training department identify those managers and supervisors who support training.

Finally, there should be room on the form for general comments that may not fit elsewhere.

# SAMPLE PARTICIPANT REACTION SHEET

Name _____     Department _____

Workshop City _____     Date _____

**Why did you attend this workshop? (check all that apply)**

___ Self development or career development
___ Selected (told to come) by someone else
___ Continuing education is a job requirement
___ Subject matter relevant to my job
___ Other (specify)

**How many years have you been involved in doing your current or similar job responsibilities?**

___ Less than one year, ___ 1–3 years, ___ 4–5 years, ___ 6–10 years, ___ 10+ years

**What was most beneficial or helpful?**

_____

_____

**What was least beneficial or helpful?**

_____

_____

**What should be added?**

_____

**What should be deleted?**

_____

**Rate each on a scale of 1 to 7 (7 = best)**

___ Instructor gave clear explanations and directions
___ Instructor listened to what I and others had to say
___ Instructor checked for understanding and summarized
___ Instructor encouraged questions and group participation
___ Instructor demonstrated knowledge and comfort with subject matter
___ Instructor encouraged me to apply the concepts presented
___ Clarity of audiovisuals
___ Value of activities and exercises
___ Value of handout book as a future resource

**Compared with other company workshops you have attended, how would you rate this program?**

___ This is my first workshop
___ One of the best
___ Very good
___ Just as good as other workshops
___ Not as good as others (Please tell us how to improve)

**How practical or useful was the information shared/learned?**

___ Extremely useful,     ___ Useful,     ___ Marginally useful,     ___ Useless

**To what extent were your personal objectives met?**

___ All met,     ___ Most met,     ___ Few met,     ___ None met

**Was the material made specific enough to your organization to be useful to you?**

___ Extremely specific

___ Specific enough

___ Only half the material applied

___ Little applied

**What is the name of the person who approved your attendance at this workshop?**

Name: _____ Title: _____

**General Comments:**

_____

_____

_____

_____

We value your opinion and thank you for taking the time to give us this information.

## Trend Analysis

The purpose of a trend analysis is to improve the design of a training program by identifying issues and problems from an analysis of several presentations of the same course. The trend analysis example on pages 188–191 compares summary information from all the presentations of a workshop during one year. Summary responses to key questions can be compared for each presentation of a workshop to monitor a trend and to identify whether a specific workshop meets a standard set by the course designer. When key questions are compared for each presentation of the course, those that fall below the acceptable standard can be investigated so the training program can be improved.

Examples of a trend analysis are shown as a bar chart (page 189) and as a scatter diagram (page 188). The course, "Survival Skills for the New Trainer," is an external vendor's public workshop with an intended target audience of trainers who have been instructing for less than a year. The workshop was presented 19 times by six different instructors throughout the United States. Field 20 on the horizontal axis ($x$ axis) is the average or mean score for all 19 sessions. The trend analysis was conducted for two key questions on this organization's Level 1 evaluation form:

1. To what extent were your personal objectives met? (Charts 1–2)

   — None met

   — Few met

   — Most met

   — All met

2. How practical or useful was the information shared and learned? (Charts 3–4)

   — Useless

   — Marginally useful

   — Useful

   — Extremely useful

Chart 1 (page 188) shows the mean data for all participants at a single presentation in answer to "How practical or useful was the information shared and learned?" as a scatter diagram. Chart 2 (page 189) shows the same data for the "practical or useful" as a bar chart. Chart 3 (page 190) shows the mean data for all participants at a single presentation in answer to "Compared to other workshops" as a bar chart. Chart 4 (page 191) shows the "To what extent were your personal objectives met" questions as a bar chart. The horizontal ($x$) axis contains the session number for that presentation of the course. The vertical ($y$) axis shows the average (mean) of all answers from a single presentation to the key question on a scale of 1 to 4.

Trend analysis allows further examination of the two presentations of this workshop that fall below the standard set by the other presentations of this workshop and can be done by asking several questions:

1. Did the same instructor present these sessions?

2. Do the participants who were less than satisfied with the workshop match the target audience for whom the course was designed?

3. Did the participants who were less than satisfied come from the same organization?

4. What do the general comments reveal about the nature of the participant's dissatisfaction?

When these questions were answered, it turns out that different instructors presented these workshops. Several of the participants were trainers with more than five years of experience. The experience level of the target population of the course is less than one year. Many of the participants were from the same company and were sent by management as a refresher. Their general comments suggested that the instructors did a "good" job of presenting information that their organization would not support, so the ideas and suggestions held little value for these participants. Based on this further analysis, no course redesign is needed.

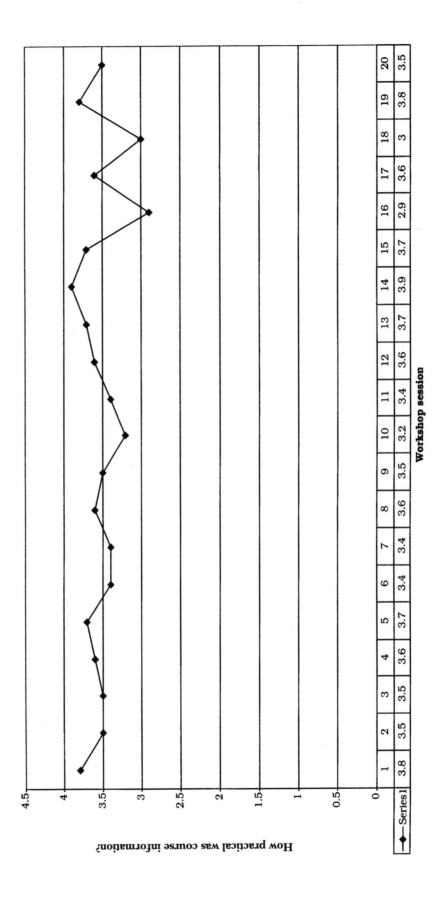

**Trend Analysis Practicality**
**Chart 1**

How practical was course information?

| | 1 | 2 | 3 | 4 | 5 | 6 | 7 | 8 | 9 | 10 | 11 | 12 | 13 | 14 | 15 | 16 | 17 | 18 | 19 | 20 |
|---|---|---|---|---|---|---|---|---|---|---|---|---|---|---|---|---|---|---|---|---|
| Series1 | 3.8 | 3.5 | 3.5 | 3.6 | 3.7 | 3.4 | 3.4 | 3.6 | 3.5 | 3.2 | 3.4 | 3.6 | 3.7 | 3.9 | 3.7 | 2.9 | 3.6 | 3 | 3.8 | 3.5 |

Workshop session

# Trend Analysis Practicality
## Chart 2

| workshop sessions | 1 | 2 | 3 | 4 | 5 | 6 | 7 | 8 | 9 | 10 | 11 | 12 | 13 | 14 | 15 | 16 | 17 | 18 | 19 | 20 |
|---|---|---|---|---|---|---|---|---|---|---|---|---|---|---|---|---|---|---|---|---|
| Series1 | 3.8 | 3.5 | 3.5 | 3.6 | 3.7 | 3.4 | 3.4 | 3.6 | 3.5 | 3.2 | 3.4 | 3.6 | 3.7 | 3.9 | 3.7 | 2.9 | 3.6 | 3 | 3.8 | 3.5 |

how practical was course information

189

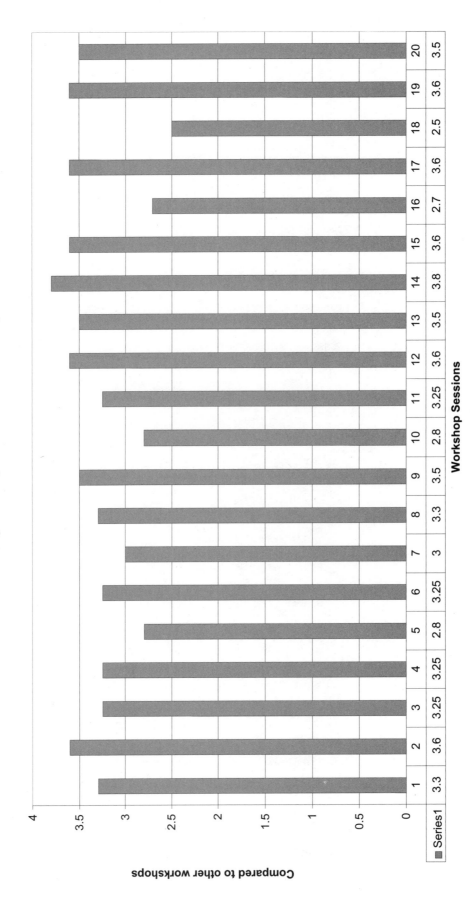

Trend Analysis Compared to Other Workshops

| | 1 | 2 | 3 | 4 | 5 | 6 | 7 | 8 | 9 | 10 | 11 | 12 | 13 | 14 | 15 | 16 | 17 | 18 | 19 | 20 |
|---|---|---|---|---|---|---|---|---|---|---|---|---|---|---|---|---|---|---|---|---|
| Series1 | 3.3 | 3.6 | 3.25 | 3.25 | 2.8 | 3.25 | 3 | 3.3 | 3.5 | 2.8 | 3.25 | 3.6 | 3.5 | 3.8 | 3.6 | 2.7 | 3.6 | 2.5 | 3.6 | 3.5 |

Workshop Sessions

Compared to other workshops

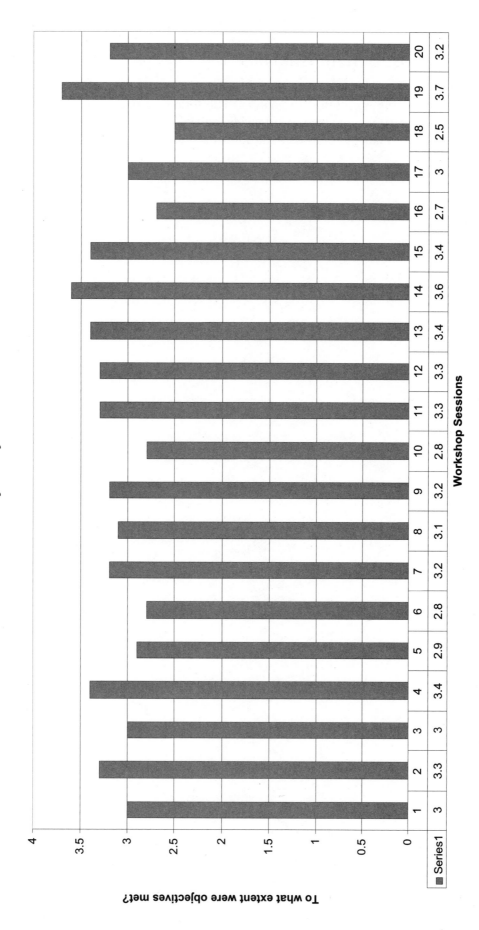

**Trend Analysis Objectives Met**

To what extent were objectives met?

Workshop Sessions

| | 1 | 2 | 3 | 4 | 5 | 6 | 7 | 8 | 9 | 10 | 11 | 12 | 13 | 14 | 15 | 16 | 17 | 18 | 19 | 20 |
|---|---|---|---|---|---|---|---|---|---|---|---|---|---|---|---|---|---|---|---|---|
| Series1 | 3 | 3.3 | 3 | 3.4 | 2.9 | 2.8 | 3.2 | 3.1 | 3.2 | 2.8 | 3.3 | 3.3 | 3.4 | 3.6 | 3.4 | 2.7 | 3 | 2.5 | 3.7 | 3.2 |

## Cost-Benefit Analysis

The second type of analysis that can help the trainer demonstrate the value of training is cost-benefit analysis. The following page is an example of a cost-benefit analysis for a Selection Interviewing workshop that was conducted for 100 retail store managers. An explanation of the analysis follows the example.

# COST-BENEFIT ANALYSIS EXAMPLE

**Training Program:** Selection Interviewing (7 hours)

**Target Population:** 100 Retail Store Managers (3 large group classes)

**Objective:** Reduce turnover of new hires by 20 percent

**TOTAL PLH** (participant learning hour) = 700 (Duration × number of participants)

·····································································

| COST | | BENEFIT |
|---|---|---|
| **Direct costs** | | **(Based on previous needs assessment)** |
| Course design | $ 9,000 | Average turn-over rate 75% |
| Instructor | 2,500 | |
| Slide-tape production | 10,000 | |
| Materials duplication | 500 | Average # clerks = 20 |
| Travel/overnight for Instructor | 1,000 | Cost to train a new clerk |
| Travel-participants | 1,000 | for 30 days = $3,000 |
| Transparencies | 50 | |
| Meals, refreshments | 3,000 | 15 new clerks per year × $3,000 = |
| | | $45,000 cost per store |
| **Total direct costs** | $27,050 | |
| **Indirect costs** | 800 | $45,000 per store |
| | | × 100 stores = $4,500,000 **lost** |
| **Total costs** | $27,850 | $4,500,000 |
| | | × .20 (target) |
| **Participant compensation** | $20,000 | $ 900,000 **benefit** |
| **Total cost** | $47,850 | $852,150 **net savings** |

PLH cost (total costs divided by PLH)    $68.36

Program cost per participant (PLH × duration) = $478.50

·····································································

## RETURN ON INVESTMENT (ROI)

$$\frac{\text{Benefit } \$900,000}{\text{Cost } \$ 47,850} = 19{:}1 \text{ BCR} \qquad \frac{\text{Net Savings } \$852,150}{\text{Cost } \$ 47,850} \times 100 = 1781\% \text{ ROI}$$

# Cost-Benefit Analysis Explanation

## Overview of Cost-Benefit Analysis

The cost-benefit analysis on the previous page is an example from one organization that wanted to reduce turnover of entry-level clerks by training managers to make better selections of employees by conducting a better selection interview.

## Cost of Current Performance

A performance analysis of the current situation revealed that store managers frequently asked existing employees for referrals for job candidates, did not adequately screen job applications, and often conducted job interviews on the sales floor. These interviews often lasted less than five minutes and the store manager used the 30-day probationary period to confirm whether a good hiring "decision" had been made. Sometimes the store manager's intuition was wrong, and the new employee would be terminated during the first 30 days of employment. This hiring practice resulted in a turnover rate in some stores of 75 percent!

The cost of recruiting, hiring and training a new employee in this organization is roughly $3000. The cost of 75 percent turnover is about $45,000 per store per year. If this sloppy hiring practice is duplicated throughout the entire chain of 100 stores, the cost could be as much as $4,500,000 per year!

## Proposed Intervention to Improve Performance

The Performance Improvement Plan proposed to conduct a *Selection Interviewing* workshop to provide skills for the managers along with a few changes in recruitment practices and a revised job application. It was also recommended that store managers train their assistants to screen the applications to save the store manager's time. Then, the store managers would have more time to conduct a more thorough interview and make a better hiring decision.

## Cost of Proposed Intervention

The cost-benefit objective of the intervention was to reduce turnover by 20 percent. Since there are several factors that can influence turnover, a modest target of 20 percent could be attributed to the successful intervention. If this objective were achieved, a projected benefit in one year would be $900,000.

## Calculating ROI

Since the cost of the training is $47,850, including participant compensation, the Benefit/Cost ratio is 19:1. This means that for every training dollar spent, the return is more than $19 back to the organization. This is a very high rate of return. If this company is publicly held, this number needs to be compared with the "earnings per share" of the company's stock. If the number is larger than the "earnings per share," then the training is worth doing.

In nonprofit, public sector or government organizations, a Benefit/Cost ratio number greater than 1 indicates that the training is worth doing. If the number is less than 1, then from a financial point of view, the training's value is questionable.

Participant compensation should be included as a cost if the employees being trained are revenue-producing employees or are employees who need to be replaced on the job by someone else while training occurs.

The form on the following page is a template for cost-benefit analysis.

# COST-BENEFIT ANALYSIS

Training program: _____

Target population: _____

Business need/objective: _____

Total participant learning hour (PLH) = duration × number of participants: _____

| *COST/INVESTMENT* | | *BENEFIT AS COST REDUCTION* |
|---|---|---|

**Direct costs**

Performance indicator** before training times number of personnel = current cost

Course design _____

Instructor _____

Performance indicator after training times number of personnel = new cost

AV materials production _____

Travel/overnight—Instructor _____

Current cost less new cost = benefit of training

Travel—participants _____

### BENEFIT AS REVENUE INCREASE

Transparencies _____

Meals, refreshments _____

Level of revenue generated by target population before training subtracted from level of revenue generated by target population after training = revenue increase (benefit of training)

Total direct costs _____

**Indirect costs** _____

**Subtotal: Total direct and indirect costs** _____

Participant compensation _____

**Total costs** _____

PLH costs (total costs ÷ PLH) = _____

Program cost per participant (PLH × duration) = _____

> **BENEFIT – TOTAL COSTS = NET SAVINGS**
> **BENEFIT TO COST RATIO (BCR) = BENEFIT ÷ COST**
> **RETURN ON INVESTMENT (ROI) = NET SAVINGS ÷ COST**

**What costs are associated with poor performance? What is the indicator of current cost of performance?

# BIBLIOGRAPHY

Balling, Carolyn, *Fit to Train*, Lakewood Books, 1997.

Barbazette, Jean, *Successful New Employee Orientation*, Pfeiffer & Assocs., 1994.

Broad, M. and J. Newstrom, *Transfer of Training*, Perseus Books, 1992.

Broadwell, Martin, *The Supervisor and On-the-Job Training*, Perseus Books, 1995.

Clark, Ruth Govin, *Developing Technical Training*, International Society for Performance Improvement, 1999.

Craig, Robert (ed.), *Training and Development Handbook* (4th ed.), McGraw-Hill, 1996.

Ellis, Steven, *How to Survive a Training Assignment*, Perseus Books, 1988.

Fisher, Sharon and Barbara Ruffino, *Establishing the Value of Training*, HRD Press, 1996.

Hart, Lois and J.G. Schleicher, *A Conference and Workshop Planner's Manual*, HRD Press, 1993.

Kayser, Thomas, *Mining Group Gold* (2d ed.), McGraw-Hill, 1995.

Kirkpatrick, Donald L., *Evaluating Training Programs: The Four Levels*, Berrett-Koehler Publishers, 1994.

Laird, Dugan, *Approaches to Training and Development* (2d ed.), Addison Wesley, 1985.

*Choosing and Using Distance Learning Options*, Lakewood Publishers, 1997.

*Lessons Learned in On-Line Training*, Lakewood Publishers, 1998.

Lucas, Robert, *The Big Book of Flip Charts*, McGraw-Hill, 1999.

Mager, Robert, *The All New Mager Six-Pack*, The Center for Effective Performance, 1997.

Mager, Robert, *Troubleshooting the Troubleshooting Course*

Newstrom, J. and Ed Scannell, *Games Trainers Play*, McGraw-Hill, 1980.

Newstrom, J. and Ed Scannell, *More Games Trainers Play*, McGraw-Hill, 1983.

Newstrom, J. and Ed Scannell, *Even More Games Trainers Play*, McGraw-Hill, 1994.

Newstrom, J. and Ed Scannell, *Still More Games Trainers Play*, McGraw-Hill, 1994.

Philips, Jack J., *Return on Investment*, Gulf Publishing Co., 1997.

Powers, Bob, *Instructor Excellence*, Jossey-Bass, 1992.

Robinson, Dana Gaines and James C. Robinson, *Performance Consulting*.

Robinson, Dana Gaines and James C. Robinson, *Training for Impact*.

Robinson, Russell D., *Helping Adults Learn and Change*.

Rothwell, William J. and H.C. Kazanas, *Mastering the Instructional Design Process*.

Silberman, Mel, *Active Training*, McGraw-Hill, 1998.

Silberman, Mel, *The Training and Performance Sourcebook,* McGraw-Hill, 1996–2001.

Stolovich, Harold and Erica Keeps (eds.), *Handbook of Human Performance Technology,* Jossey-Bass, 1992.

Trepper, Charles H., *Training for Software Rollouts,* McGraw-Hill, 2000.

Zemke, Ron, *Figuring Things Out.*

# Appendix A

# TRAINING DEPARTMENT AUDIT

The opening questions from each chapter are repeated here in summary form to provide the trainer with an opportunity to audit all the functions addressed in the following 38 questions. Five stages of development are identified for the functions. The five stages of development are

1. Aimed at short-term results

2. Requirements have been defined

3. Aimed at effective use of internal expertise

4. Aimed at systematic improvement

5. Aimed at continuous improvement

After completing the audit by rating the stage of development for all 38 questions, the trainer can create an action plan to identify which areas of development are appropriate for the training function. Refer back to each chapter for suggestions when seeking to move to the next stage of development.

## Chapter 1: Prioritize Training Responsibilities

1. *Which stage of development describes how priorities are set for the training coordinator?*

   — Stage 1: How to set priorities is unclear. You are reactive and focus on administrative functions. Roles and responsibilities are sometimes unclear and overlap with other areas.

   — Stage 2: You have a written job description and a specific line of reporting authority. Much of your work consists of "other duties as assigned."

   — Stage 3: Your priorities are to act primarily as an internal consultant to management, to find resources for courses, to select and develop internal subject matter experts as trainers, and to select appropriate external trainers and training packages. Your roles and responsibilities are clear to you and others.

   — Stage 4: You do everything described in Stage 3 and find back-up instructors to avoid canceling classes during highly active training periods.

   — Stage 5: You do everything described in Stage 4 and also assure the function addresses appropriate issues by using continuous improvement methods.

2. *Which stage of development describes the mission and objectives of the training function?*

   — Stage 1: There is no clearly defined mission or business plan. If a mission statement exists, it is not clearly communicated internally to management.

   — Stage 2: The mission and objectives are clearly defined for the staff by upper management and limited to products and or services.

   — Stage 3: The training function mission and objectives are developed into a training plan.

   — Stage 4: Progress toward achieving the mission and objectives of the training function is regularly assessed.

   — Stage 5: When necessary, the mission and objectives are adjusted based on information from a variety of resources.

## Chapter 2: Gain Support for the Training Department

3. *Describe the level of access and support for training from upper management.*

   — Stage 1: The training department operates on a reactive basis to assist upper management with immediate operational requests.

   — Stage 2: The training department takes initial steps to gain access to management to support individual training events with minimal planning.

   — Stage 3: Management is accessible on a regular basis to the training department and those who train. Management shows a real interest in training and often introduces training events.

— Stage 4: Management is accessible and supportive of training projects.

— Stage 5: Management is directly accessible and supportive and participates as a sponsor for training department projects.

4. *Describe how well you keep up to date with training trends.*

— Stage 1: I have no awareness of training trends.

— Stage 2: I have minimal awareness of training trends.

— Stage 3: Trend updates are pursued on an individual basis.

— Stage 4: Training trends are systematically studied and followed where appropriate.

— Stage 5: Training trends updates are integrated into doing business. The training department is a trendsetter and may participate in trend research. Planning helps to avoid negative consequences of impending trends.

5. *Describe the level of support for trainers to participate in professional organizations.*

— Stage 1: Little or no support exists for membership in outside professional organizations.

— Stage 2: Attendance at outside training and professional meetings is limited due to work pressure.

— Stage 3: Training professionals occasionally attend outside professional development sessions and share that information with colleagues.

— Stage 4: Training professionals regularly attend outside professional development sessions and share that information with colleagues.

— Stage 5: Active membership in professional organizations is normal. Trainers are trendsetters among their peers and give presentations at professional conferences.

6. *Describe the level of decision-making authority and appreciation expressed by management for the duties and responsibilities of the training department.*

— Stage 1: Management gives little to no decision-making authority with training responsibilities.

— Stage 2: Management gives minor decision-making authority along with training responsibilities.

— Stage 3: Management gives regular training-related decision-making authority to the training department for routine responsibilities. Training professionals make recommendations for how to handle new responsibilities.

— Stage 4: Management gives regular training-related decision-making authority to training professionals for all responsibilities and seeks approval for unusual decisions.

— Stage 5: Management gives all training-related decision-making authority to the training department. The training professional reports exceptions to management after the event has passed.

## Chapter 3: How to Assess Training Needs

7. *What is assessed and how?*

— Stage 1: No clear process to assess needs is evident.

— Stage 2: Tasks are analyzed to determine the appropriate way to teach a task. Performance analysis is used. Training needs are sorted from training wants.

— Stage 3: Learning needs of a target population are identified with client involvement. Goal analysis is used to clarify vague training needs. Course materials and appropriate training methodologies are linked to the needs of the target population.

— Stage 4: Course materials and methodologies are appropriate and valid.

— Stage 5: There is strong cooperation between the client and the training department to integrate business needs, training needs, specific targets, and job standards.

8. *How is needs assessment done?*

— Stage 1: Scheduling of existing training courses substitutes for needs assessment.

— Stage 2: Task analysis is done to teach a standardized process.

— Stage 3: A resource requirements analysis is done to identify the most cost-effective and appropriate method(s) to present training.

— Stage 4: The needs for new learning and course updates are reviewed on a scheduled basis. Line managers are taught to assess training needs and regularly share information with the training department.

— Stage 5: There is strong cooperation between the client and the training department to integrate business needs, training needs, specific targets, and job standards.

9. *What is the product of the assessment and how are assessments tied to business needs?*

— Stage 1: A schedule of training events is created. No specific tie to a business need is evident.

— Stage 2: Clear learning outcomes are identified and tied to how a job is done.

— Stage 3: A training plan is developed to include clearly defined business issues that require support from training. Training needs and wants are sorted, and a means to evaluate the training is recommended.

— Stage 4: Executives are interviewed regularly to identify business needs that require the support of training and for long-term objectives.

— Stage 5: There is strong cooperation between the client and the training department to integrate business needs, training needs, specific targets, and job standards.

10. *What is the training professional's role in needs assessment?*

— Stage 1: None.

— Stage 2: The trainer attends client's staff meetings to stay current on impending needs and to identify future needs.

— Stage 3: The trainer acts as an internal consultant and identifies how needs have changed over time and identifies new needs.

— Stage 4: The training professional acts as an internal consultant and systematically identifies how needs have changed and identifies new needs.

— Stage 5: There is strong cooperation between the client and the training department to integrate business needs, training needs, specific targets, and job standards.

11. *What is the extent of planning for training?*

— Stage 1: None.

— Stage 2: Training needs and wants are sorted. The training professional helps the operation identify training needs.

— Stage 3: A training plan is completed in response to specific requests and covers conducting one or a few training programs. Training costs are identified and more than one resource is identified for selection of the best alternative.

— Stage 4: A training plan is created for a year at a time in response to a variety of training requests that anticipates training needs.

— Stage 5: Training partners with operations to identify training needs that are tied to business needs. The annual planning process has input from operations, training and customers.

## Chapter 4: How to Select Training Programs and Packages

12. *How are packaged training programs selected?*

— Stage 1: There are no clear criteria for the selection of training packages.

— Stage 2: Selection criteria are clear. Proposals are requested to compare similar packages. References are checked.

— Stage 3: Packaged training programs are reviewed as needed with input from internal clients and measured against criteria.

— Stage 4: A systematic process exists for gathering resources, reviewing and selecting training packages with input from internal clients, and measuring them against criteria.

— Stage 5: In addition to accomplishing what is done in Stage 4, each request for a new program is matched to the changing needs of the organization.

## Chapter 5: Select and Coach Subject Matter Experts as Trainers

13. *Which stage of development describes how subject matter experts are selected as internal trainers?*

    — Stage 1: No clear criteria exist for the selection of subject matter experts as internal trainers.

    — Stage 2: Selection criteria for subject matter experts as internal trainers are clear. Trainers usually have high subject matter expertise and recent field experience.

    — Stage 3: Written requirements for subject matter experts as internal trainers cover knowledge of subject matter, training skills, and practical expertise in the field.

    — Stage 4: A formal assessment process has subject matter experts demonstrate knowledge, training skills, and practical expertise in the field.

    — Stage 5: In addition to Stage 4, subject matter experts have demonstrated ability to relate learning and training to organizational business needs.

14. *Which stage of development describes how internal trainers get feedback?*

    — Stage 1: Internal trainers receive no formal feedback, although some may solicit informal feedback from learners.

    — Stage 2: Feedback is received randomly and only occasionally from the line supervisor or trainer. Some feedback is provided from written participant end-of-course evaluations.

    — Stage 3: Internal trainers get regular feedback from the line supervisor, the trainer, and participants' evaluations.

    — Stage 4: Internal trainer competencies are regularly assessed through end-of-course evaluations and visits by on-site trainers and/or line supervisors. Training skills are assessed during performance appraisals.

    — Stage 5: Feedback and trend analysis are used extensively.

15. *Which stage of development describes how internal trainers improve their skills?*

    — Stage 1: Internal trainers received no train-the-trainer skill development.

    — Stage 2: Internal trainers develop training skills on their own.

    — Stage 3: Internal trainers are encouraged to attend outside train-the-trainer courses. An occasional in-house train-the-trainer course may be offered.

    — Stage 4: Internal trainers receive systematic development by practical experience in their subject area. Most SMEs share time between training and other duties.

— Stage 5: Internal trainers get knowledge, practical training, and field experience for continuous improvement.

16. *Which stage of development describes methodologies used by internal trainers?*

— Stage 1: Internal trainers' methods are limited to lecture, large group discussion, demonstration and practice sessions.

— Stage 2: Internal trainers' methods include adult learning techniques.

— Stage 3: Internal trainers' methods include appropriate participation, pacing and discovery learning.

— Stage 4: Internal trainers use a variety of training methods to enhance the effectiveness of training.

— Stage 5: Internal trainers use state-of-the-art methods to help meet the business need through training.

## Chapter 6: How to Keep Training Courses Up to Date

17. *Which stage of development describes how courses are maintained?*

— Stage 1: No systematic maintenance of courses exists. Trainers often use technical manuals in place of handout materials.

— Stage 2: One subject matter expert or trainer becomes responsible for course maintenance of a purchased course. Internal course refinements imitate the external vendor's methods.

— Stage 3: Key subject matter experts (SMEs) or trainers are responsible for course maintenance with input from others.

— Stage 4: Key SMEs are responsible for course maintenance and systematically ask for input from others.

— Stage 5: Key SMEs are responsible for course maintenance through research, trend analysis and input from other SMEs and internal customers.

18. *Which stage of development describes leader or facilitator guides used by internal trainers?*

— Stage 1: No lesson plan or facilitator guide exists.

— Stage 2: A leader's guide is provided by external vendors.

— Stage 3: Leader's guides are developed internally in an outline format.

— Stage 4: Leader's guides are developed internally, and format is based on assessment of the course and the instructor's needs.

— Stage 5: Leaders guides are developed and improved internally based on an ongoing assessment and feedback from users.

19. *Which stage of development describes the multiple roles of internal trainers?*

— Stage 1: Technical trainers complete testing and certification to present subject in their expertise.

— Stage 2: Internal trainers are segregated into those who instruct and those who instruct and update courses.

— Stage 3: Trainers are cross-trained to present multiple programs. All trainers give input for course revisions. External trainers are limited to new course development beyond internal expertise.

— Stage 4: Key trainers systematically identify business needs and the effects of training.

— Stage 5: Training needs are aligned with business needs and courses are evaluated for bottom line results. Results are routinely reported to management.

# Chapter 7: How to Hire a Consultant or External Trainer

20. *Which stage of development describes how external consultants are selected?*

— Stage 1: No clear selection criteria or means exist.

— Stage 2: Selection criteria are clear. Consultants usually have high subject matter expertise and recent parallel client experience.

— Stage 3: Written external consultant requirements contain knowledge of subject matter, training, and process skills and practical expertise in the field.

— Stage 4: Consulting candidates demonstrate knowledge, skills and expertise in a formal assessment process.

— Stage 5: In addition to stage 4 development, external consultants skills are related to the organization's business needs.

# Chapter 8: How to Begin to Market Training Internally

21. *Which stage of development describes how training is marketed in the organization?*

— Stage 1: The training function "sells" courses to internal clients from existing products or services.

— Stage 2: The training function investigates the need for training and selects courses designed to meet the business need.

— Stage 3: The training function conducts a regular needs assessment to be sure training courses are meeting the current needs.

— Stage 4: The training function systematically uses a marketing approach to providing training services.

— Stage 5: The training function partners with operations to update existing courses and find new resources and always promotes training that meets the business need.

22. *Which stage of development describes the extent and variety of the marketing effort?*

— Stage 1: The training function makes no effort to promote training beyond the person or group who requests the event or course.

— Stage 2: The training function uses a variety of methods to attract those who might benefit from scheduled training.

— Stage 3: The training function uses various methods that demonstrate the benefits of training to the learner and how to use what is learned, while promoting the event at least three months before it occurs.

— Stage 4: The training function systematically enlists help from supervisors to promote training, has personal ambassadors promote training with testimonials, and publishes successes of past training participants.

— Stage 5: The training function partners with supervisors and line managers to improve awareness of training events. Unique methods promote training including learning contracts, open house, events, and publishing the function's training plan.

## Chapter 9: How to Publicize Training Events

23. *Which stage of development describes the use of training brochures and catalogs?*

— Stage 1: The training department creates a brief announcement for existing training, published through e-mail, and announces training events at regular meetings.

— Stage 2: The training department prepares individual brochures to identify when and where training will be held. Newsletters and bulletin boards also announce training events along with e-mail and the supervisor's assistance.

— Stage 3: The training department publishes a course catalog of offerings on at least a quarterly basis. Offerings identify the target audience, benefits of training, and how to enroll. The training department maintains a Web page that promotes training.

— Stage 4: Training brochures and catalogs include testimonials and successes of past participants. Pictures, graphics, and a training department logo create a signature look in promotional materials. Employees can register on-line or via fax, telephone, or mail.

— Stage 5: The training department's branding is extensively used to promote programs. Feedback on the success of different marketing materials is tracked. Trend analysis identifies which brochures are most successful.

24. *What is the stage of development for the methods used to publicize training events?*

— Stage 1: Little to no means are used to publicize training events. Employees are often notified on the day of training to attend a specific program.

— Stage 2: Training events are publicized through memo and e-mail announcements to the target population.

— Stage 3: Each training event is publicized using a variety of methods such as brochures, bulletin boards, letters of invitation, staff meeting announcements, memos, and e-mails.

— Stage 4: A systematic approach is used in partnership with supervisors and managers to publicize events both individually and clustered.

— Stage 5: In addition to the systematic approach used at Stage 4, creative and innovative methods are used to promote training, such as contests, incentives, and use of personal ambassadors in each department.

## Chapter 10: How to Set Up and Maintain Your Company's Training Web Site

25.  *Which stage of development describes the type of training information on your Web page?*

— Stage 1: The training department does not have a Web page.

— Stage 2: The training department posts information on the organization's intranet, but does not have its own Web page.

— Stage 3: The training department has its own Web page that describes the content and objectives of its workshops and other services.

— Stage 4: The training department's Web page is systematically maintained and updated on a regular basis.

— Stage 5: The training function's Web page is continually improved with links to other sites, new features, activities, resources and benefits.

## Chapter 11: How to Smoothly Administer Training Events

26.  *Which stage of development describes how your training department selects courses and plans for specific training events?*

— Stage 1: Administrative procedures are developed for each project on a one-time basis.

— Stage 2: A list of courses describes training offerings. Listings are posted on bulletin boards and/or the organization's intranet.

— Stage 3: A catalog details course offerings. Productivity statistics are used in a limited manner to identify the need for training. Training paths are established for only a few select technical target populations.

— Stage 4: Productivity statistics are used to identify training needs. Training paths are established for all target populations.

— Stage 5: Procedures are in place to ensure the integrity of the scheduling process, respond to user requests, and deal with complaints and unforeseen needs. Business cycles dictate the training schedule for off-peak times.

27.  *How are courses scheduled?*

— Stage 1: Courses are scheduled based on requests from the field or dictate of upper management.

— Stage 2: Courses are scheduled based on the target population's anticipated needs.

— Stage 3: Training is scheduled from a systematic assessment of the target population's needs.

— Stage 4: Course schedules are based on information collected from the client's current and anticipated needs.

— Stage 5: Procedures are in place to ensure the integrity of the scheduling process, respond to user requests, and deal with complaints and unforeseen needs. Business cycles dictate the training schedule for off-peak times.

28. *Describe the extent to which statistics are used in the scheduling process.*

— Stage 1: No statistics are used to schedule training.

— Stage 2: New course offerings are scheduled based on management dictate or industry requirements.

— Stage 3: Data is collected and analyzed from training needs listed on the employees' performance appraisals and other needs analysis.

— Stage 4: Statistical analysis of instructor productivity assures equitable work assignments and scheduling of a trainer's classroom sessions, preparation, course development, and travel time.

— Stage 5: Procedures are in place to ensure the integrity of the scheduling process, respond to user requests, and deal with complaints and unforeseen needs. Business cycles dictate the training schedule for off-peak times.

29. *Describe the registration, record-keeping, and confirmation systems for your training department.*

— Stage 1: Minimal clerical support is focused on enrollment, registration, record keeping, and travel requirements of trainers and participants.

— Stage 2: Minimal attendance and minimal reporting are done when requested.

— Stage 3: A statistical specialist keeps training data that is available and regularly reports activities to management.

— Stage 4: Statistical data is formatted, interpreted, and distributed within the department for productivity analysis.

— Stage 5: Statistical data is formatted, interpreted, and distributed to training users to demonstrate how the business needs are met. Administrative support explores alternative methods to report training data.

30. *How are classrooms prepared and materials support accomplished?*

— Stage 1: Instructors prepare classrooms and provide materials for their courses.

— Stage 2: Administrative support prepares classrooms and keeps an inventory of course materials.

— Stage 3: Administrative support provides for participant materials and word processing and duplication of the leader's guide.

— Stage 4: Administrative support regularly anticipates and provides for the needs of internal and external trainers and participants.

— Stage 5: Administrative support exceeds the expectations of internal and external trainers and participants. Quality and format of training materials are continually updated to be on a par with what is available commercially.

31. *What additional support services are available to your training function?*

— Stage 1: No additional support services are provided.

— Stage 2: Specific guidelines from trainer and participants are drafted, and commitments to projects are met on a limited basis.

— Stage 3: A specialist is available to develop color transparencies, custom graphics, PowerPoint presentations, etc.

— Stage 4: Specialized requests based on individual trainer needs or management are met.

— Stage 5: Specialized services are tailored to meet the needs of target groups and internal customers.

# Chapter 12: How to Set Up Off-Site Training Events

32. *Which stage of development describes how your training department selects and deals with off-site training facilities for specific training events?*

— Stage 1: No outside facilities are used.

— Stage 2: Outside facilities are used on an as needed basis without any set system.

— Stage 3: Requirements for off-site facilities are clearly communicated, and at least two facilities are contacted for competitive bids.

— Stage 4: Requirements are systematically met by one or two off-site facilities with regular feedback provided to keep service at a highly satisfactory level.

— Stage 5: We partner with off-site facilities to meet a variety of needs and have a continuous improvement process in place.

33. *Which stage of development describes how your training department makes travel arrangements for instructors and participants?*

— Stage 1: The training department makes no travel arrangements. Instructors and participants make their own travel arrangements.

— Stage 2: The corporate travel department—or an external travel agent—makes arrangements as needed for instructors and participants.

— Stage 3: The training department recommends specific hotels, airlines, and rental car companies with which corporate rates have been arranged.

— Stage 4: The training department makes or coordinates with the travel agent hotel, car rental, and air travel reservations from preferences identified in the traveler's profile.

— Stage 5: The training department makes or coordinates with the travel agent all travel arrangements, including ground transfers and airport pickup service, and constantly strives to improve the level of service.

## Chapter 13: Set Up and Run a Corporate Resource Center

34. *Which stage of development describes how your training function selects and maintains audiovisual equipment?*

— Stage 1: No clear criteria exist for the selection of audiovisual equipment.

— Stage 2: Selection criteria are clear. Proposals are requested to compare similar equipment. References are checked.

— Stage 3: Equipment specifications are written, and proposals are reviewed with input from internal clients.

— Stage 4: A systematic process exists for gathering resources and reviewing and selecting training equipment, with input from internal clients, against written criteria. Shared use of equipment is encouraged where appropriate.

— Stage 5: A systematic process exists for gathering resources and reviewing and selecting training equipment, with input from internal clients, against written criteria. Shared use of equipment is encouraged where appropriate. Each request for a new piece of equipment is matched with the changing needs of the organization.

35. *Which stage of development describes how your training function provides support services and acts as a resource center for the organization?*

— Stage 1: No additional support services are offered.

— Stage 2: Specific guidelines from trainers and participants are met on a limited basis.

— Stage 3: A specialist is available to develop color transparencies, custom graphics, PowerPoint presentations, etc. Guidelines exist to access resources provided by the training department.

— Stage 4: Specialized requests, based on individual needs of trainers or management, are systematically met.

— Stage 5: Specialized services are tailored to meet the needs of target groups and clients.

## Chapter 14: Show Me the Money: Budgeting for Training

36. *Which stage of development describes how your training function identifies the feasibility of conducting training?*

— Stage 1: No feasibility analysis is done.

— Stage 2: An estimate of training costs is created prior to each training event.

— Stage 3: A budget is developed that identifies the cost of training and the benefits expected from conducting the training.

— Stage 4: A training budget is created systematically. Unanticipated training events require a feasibility analysis prior to approval.

— Stage 5: Statistics are used to demonstrate the results of training, are compared with the feasibility analysis, and are a regular part of the budgeting process.

## Chapter 15: How to Evaluate and Demonstrate the Success of Training

37. *Which stage of development describes how your training department evaluates participant reactions to training events?*

— Stage 1: No evaluation formal is performed or the instructor performs evaluation only informally.

— Stage 2: A checklist with ratings asks for participant's reactions, level of satisfaction with the content, and skill of the instructor.

— Stage 3: A summary report is created from participant's reactions and provided to the instructor and the internal customer.

— Stage 4: A summary report is shared with the instructor, the internal customer, and the course designer to systematically improve the content and process of instruction.

— Stage 5: Trend analysis incorporates summary information to continuously improve the content and process of instruction.

38. *Which stage of development describes how the results of training are measured?*

— Stage 1: No results are measured.

— Stage 2: No results are measured, but instructors or supervisors may collect informal information about the results of training.

— Stage 3: The trainer and/or supervisor identifies the costs associated with the development and delivery of training.

— Stage 4: The trainer and/or supervisor creates a cost-benefit analysis to identify the bottom line impact and how well training met the business need associated with each course. The training department measures training outcomes against the training plan.

— Stage 5: The training department relates the cost-benefit analysis to the business need, and revises the training plan as appropriate with input from the client.

# Appendix B

# TRAINING RESOURCES

This appendix contains a variety of training resources:

- Web pages

- Consultant directories

- Workshop listing and registration services

- Training associations

## Web Sites

Lakewood Publications: *www.trainingsupersite.com*

National Library of Congress: *http://marvel.loc.gov*

Instructional technology site with links to others:
*www.cudenver.edu/~mryder/itcon.html*

The Training Clinic: *www.thetrainingclinic.com*

Successful Meetings Magazine: *www.successmtgs.com*

Training Statistics and Benchmarking: *www.nwlink.com/~donclark/hrd/trainsta.html*

## Consultant Directories

Consultants Mall: *http://www.consultants-mall.com/consult2.htm*

Consulting Central: *http://www.consultingcentral.com/*

Most of the training associations have a consultant directory.

## Seminar Web Sites

First Seminar Service (978) 452-0766 *www.trinq.com*

Seminar Finder (805) 563-7731 *www.seminarfinder.com*

Seminar Information Service (949) 261-9104 *www.seminarinformation.com*

Training Registry *www.trainingregistry.com*

Training Central (781) 235-8095 *www.tscentral.com*

Training and Seminar Locater (TASL) *www.tasl.com/tasl/home/html*

## Training Associations

**American Society for Healthcare Education and Training (ASHET)**
(Part of American Hospital Assn.)
One N. Franklin Street, Chicago, IL 60606
(National Conference, June each year)

**American Society for Training and Development (ASTD)**
Membership Services, P.O. Box 1567, Merrifield, VA 22116-9812
(703) 683-8100 (National Conference, May or June each year), www.astd.org

**Association for Experiential Education**
www.aee.org

**Association for Quality and Participation**
801-B West 8th St., Suite 501, Cincinnati, Ohio 45203
(513) 381-1959 www.aqp.org

**Credit Union National Association (CUNA)**
Helps measure return on investment of training (ROI) www.cuna.org/data/news
    now/spec_reports/cpd/cpd4.html

**Digital Learning Organization**
901 Burlington Avenue, Ste. 2, Western Springs, IL 60558 (877) 533-4914
www.digitallearning.org

**Distance Education Clearinghouse**
Run by the University of Wisconsin www.usex.edu/disted/home.html

**Electronic Performance Support Systems (EPSS)**
www.epss.com

**International Association for Human Resource Information Management, Inc.**
P. O. Box 801646, Dallas, TX 75380-1646 (972) 661-3727 www.ihrim.org

**International Federation of Training & Development Organizations (IFTDO)**
7 Westbourne Road, Southport PR8-2HZ, England
Contact: David Wake (44) (704) 67994
(International training conference each summer) www.iftdo.org

**International Society for Performance Improvement (ISPI formerly NSPI)**
1300 L Street NW, Suite 1250, Washington DC 20005
(202) 408-7969 (National Conference, March/April each year)
www.ispi.org

**Learning Technologies Library**
Office of Learning Technology, HRD Canada
http://olt-bta.crdc-drhc.gc.ca/info/index.html

**National Association of Government Training and Development Directors (NAGTADD)**
167 W. Main St., Suite 600, Lexington, KY 40607, 606-231-1948 tel, 606-231-1928
    fax
E-mail: Meredith Cash *Meridmeredithc@bop.state.sd.us*

**National Environmental Training Association**
3020 East Camelback, Suite 399, Phoenix, AZ 85016-4421
(602) 956-6099 (National Conference, August each year)

**Ontario Society for Training and Development**
110 Richmond Street East, Suite 206
Toronto, Ontario M5C 1P1, Canada, (416) 367-5900

**Organizational Development Network (ODN)**
76 S. Orange Avenue, Suite 101, South Orange, NJ 07079-1923
(201) 763-7337 (Several Annual Conferences) www.odnet.org

**Society of Human Resource Management (SHRM formerly ASPA)**
1800 Duke Street, Alexandria, VA 22314-3499
(703) 548-3440, (800) 238-7476 (National Conference, June each year)
www.shrm.org

**Society of Insurance Trainers and Educators (SITE)**
2120 Market Street, Suite 108, San Francisco, CA 94114

(415) 621-2830, fax: (415) 621-0889, socinstred@aol.com
(National Conference, June each year)

**Trainers Association of Southern California (TASC)**
P. O. Box 51534, Irvine, CA 92619-1534 (714) 893-3929
http://wam.bpfa.com/trainers
Trainers involved in computer technology. Chapters in Los Angeles, Orange Co.,
    and San Diego

**Training & Development Community Center (TCM)**
www.tcm.com

**United States Distance Learning Association**
P. O. Box 5129, San Ramon, CA 94583 (925)606-5160, fax: (925) 606-9410
Teleconferencing events from around the world www.usdla.org

**Web Based Training Information Center**
www.filename.com/wbt/index.html

## Appendix C

# FIVE STEPS OF ADULT LEARNING

This is a general description of what takes place during the five steps of adult learning. Adults need to progress through these five steps for any type of activity, including a lecture.

1. **Instructor sets up the learning activity**

   To be successful, any learning experience needs a setup so the participants understand what they are going to do and why they are doing it. Adult learners become motivated when they understand the benefit or importance of the activity to themselves. Directions and ground rules are usually included regarding how the learning activity is to be conducted. Setup can include such things as

   ☐ Tell participants the purpose of the activity

   ☐ Divide participants into groups

   ☐ Assign roles

   ☐ Give the ground rules

   ☐ Explain what the participants are going to do

   ☐ Tell why they are doing the activity without giving away what is to be "discovered"

2. **Learning activity**

   For a learning activity to be successful, an adult needs to be involved as much as possible. It is also appropriate to consider how the activity will appeal to the senses of sight, hearing, and touch. This step includes any learning activity such as

   ☐ Lecture

   ☐ Case study

   ☐ Session starter

   ☐ Small group work

   ☐ Role play

   ☐ Participation activity

   ☐ Questionnaire

   ☐ Simulation, instructional game

   ☐ Inventory

3. **Learners share and interpret their reactions to the activity**

   This step is essential to help conclude the activity and help learners identify what happened during the activity. It is meant to help the learner analyze the activity and then develop individual and group reactions to the activity. Learners share their reactions by identifying what happened to themselves, others, and how his or her behavior affected others. Often questions are asked such as, "What was your partner's reaction when you did . . .?" or "What helped or hindered your progress?" or "Summarize the key points from the lecture, role play, or case study."

Sometimes, it is appropriate to have each participant write down his or her reaction so that another person does not influence it before sharing it.

Sharing a reaction is the beginning step of developing a pattern. If some participants do not share their reactions, it is difficult to "end the activity," and they may prolong some unfinished business that spills over into other activities during the workshop.

4. **Learners identify concepts from their reactions**

This is the "so what did I learn" step. Questions that develop concepts include, "What did you learn about how to conduct an interview, discipline a subordinate, teach a new job, etc." If this step is left out, then learning will be incomplete. Participants will have been entertained, but may not be able to apply new learning to similar situations outside the classroom. When concepts are inferred from an activity, adult learners are ready to apply these newly learned or recently confirmed concepts to future situations.

5. **Learners apply concepts to their situation**

This is the "so what now" step. Adult learners are asked to use and apply new information learned from the activity and confirmed through a discussion of general concepts to their situation. This often involves an action step such as "How will you use this questioning technique the next time a subordinate asks you for a favor?" or "In what types of situations would you be more effective if you used this technique?" If this step is left out, then the learner may not see the relationship between the learning activity and his or her job or situation, and consider what was learned by others as not useful to him or her.

# INDEX

## About the Author

Jean Barbazette (Seal Beach, CA) is president and founder of The Training Clinic, a training and consulting firm. A popular presenter, she has conducted workshops at many national and international training conferences. She is the author of the best-selling *Successful New Employee Orientation*.